How to Avoid the Divorce from Hell*

*And dance together
at your daughter's wedding

How to Avoid the Divorce from Hell*

M. SUE TALIA

*and dance together at your daughter's wedding

Nexus Publishing Company
Danville, California

For more information, please contact Nexus Publishing Company,
2333 San Ramon Valley Boulevard, Suite 150, San Ramon, California, 94583-1613.

First printing 1996.

Although the author and publisher have made every effort to ensure the accuracy and completeness of the information contained in this book, we assume no responsibility for errors, inaccuracies, omissions, or any inconsistency herein. Any slights of people, places or organizations are unintentional.

The quote of Lucy Van Pelt from "Peanuts" is used with permission of Charles M. Schultz and United Media.

ISBN 0-9651075-0-7

LCCN 96-70252

Cover and interior design by Allen M. Crider

Photograph by Roger Varon

Printed by Malloy Lithographing, Inc.

To Lee,

who came home one night and told me about a new client he had seen that day. She wasn't ready to file for divorce yet, but wanted to know if there was a book she could read to learn about the process. He told her a good friend of his was writing it. She just didn't know it yet.

Thanks for the countless hours spent trying to figure out how to make the system work better for parents and kids, how to reduce conflict and help people solve their differences with dignity.

Thanks for the inspiration . . .

Contents

Preface

So, you're contemplating a divorce. Like anyone else in your position, you are frantically looking for books, instructions and other resources to help you navigate the rapids you are entering. This book is designed to do just that.

Although I have been a divorce lawyer for many years, this book is not just about law. Its purpose is to let you know that despite the fact that the divorce process is foreign, grindingly slow, intensely painful and frustrating, you have a great deal more control over it than you probably realize. You are not solely at the mercy of your spouse, the lawyers and a stranger in a black robe. Just as the choices you have made throughout your life have brought you to the point where you are charting this new course, you have choices to make at the outset of the case and at hundreds of forks in the path thereafter. Those decisions will largely determine the degree to which you experience either pain and frustration on one hand or growth and renewal on the other.

If you choose to commence an adversarial procedure, consumed with hostility toward your spouse, I guarantee that hostility will be returned in spades. Instead, if you commit to steering through the process as cleanly as possible, the rewards will be manifold.

Something is not working in your life. If everything were perfect, you would not be reading this book. You are obviously considering making some major changes, changes which however difficult, you believe will improve the quality of your life. I am here to tell you that the process can be constructive, cleansing and, oddly enough, positive. It is possible to come out on the other side, look yourself in the mirror and know in your heart and in your soul that you did the best you could, that you did nothing to contribute to your own or another's pain, and that when you made a mistake, you corrected and learned from it. We can ask nothing more from life.

Divorce, by definition, involves a man and a woman. The impact of gender is unavoidable. In order to avoid the cumbersome he/she, I have chosen to use gender-based pronouns interchangeably. An example referring to how "she" reacts may just as well mean "he."

You may find the same subject woven through several chapters. Many readers will use this book as a resource and consult isolated chapters rather than going cover to cover, and I want the discussion to be complete. In other instances, the topic is just so important that I want to be sure it isn't missed.

This book is the product of 18 years as a divorce lawyer. It is designed for the ninety percent of divorcing couples who are basically sane, reasonable people who want to get through the process as whole and unscarred as possible.

Most people facing divorce are terrified. The system is public, cumbersome and impersonal. They must put their faith in strangers whom they hire to protect their interests and guide them through a dizzying maze of legal concepts. The very fabric of their lives is ripping, from where they live to how often they see their children to whether they can pay their bills. This book is designed to give them the tools to make good decisions as they wend their way through the process.

It is not designed to give legal advice. That is for the lawyers. Neither is it a substitute for a therapist. Most importantly, it is not intended to replace your own judgment. Each person is responsible for the manner in which he processes this, and any other experience.

Ultimately, each of us faces divorce, as any other life-transforming process, as an individual. We are the sum of our past experiences and imprinting, and the process will not be the same for any two people. Each of you must decide what works for you and discard what doesn't.

As you read the following pages, many of you will have no difficulty seeing your spouse. Do yourself a favor. Be honest and look again to see if you find yourself as well.

I have made a number of suggestions you can use to make good decisions. You can choose to make the process a healthy, growth-inducing passage or a dig a bitter, vengeful pit in which you wallow for the rest of your life. Choose wisely.

Part I

Getting Started: Introduction to Reality Testing

Choices — the Divorce Everyone Wants

Of course you want your divorce to be amicable. Only a lunatic would prefer to sit across a courtroom and battle the person with whom she shared a bed for 5, 10 or 20 years. What parent in his right mind would choose to subject his children to the trauma and uncertainty of a custody fight? In 18 years, I've found that most new clients start out with a variation of "Now, I want this to be amicable." So, what goes wrong? Lots of things. People let their fears take charge and act in ways the other party, equally frightened, perceives as hostile. Friends and family take sides and inject their own agendas, polarizing the situation. A parent who doesn't really want a custody fight starts a defensive one because he's afraid that if he doesn't fight for custody, the kids will think he doesn't want them, or worse, that if he doesn't have custody he won't see them.

Is it possible to have a successful divorce?

The good news is that yes, it is possible. It isn't easy, and requires maturity and commitment to the goal, but it is possible.

Every divorce is a compendium of choices, both past and present. If you and your spouse decided that one of you should stay home and raise the children, that is going to have far-reaching impact on custody, child and spousal support rights and obligations. If you are the one who stayed home, that decision will impact your present and future career opportunities. If you lived beyond your means as an intact family, the split into two households will create a true financial hardship. All these choices are part of the fabric as it exists when you first decide to divorce.

So, what can *you* do to pull it off, to have a successful divorce? You have options which, if exercised wisely, will substantially increase your chances of success.

- Commit to keep lines of communication with your spouse as open as possible.

- To the extent you can, separate your feelings of hurt, guilt or rejection from decisions regarding property, money or, for God's sake, the kids.

- Try to remember that even if you can no longer live together, you once loved and respected your spouse enough to marry her in the first place, probably to have children with her. Remember that you are *both* human and are entitled to your dignity.

- Divorce doesn't happen in a vacuum, and, just as it takes two to make a marriage, it takes two to make a divorce. Each of you must accept some responsibility for the chain of events which brought you to this point. You each must also accept responsibility for your own conduct through the divorce.

- Realize that whatever pain you are feeling, your spouse is probably experiencing comparable, though equally unique and personalized, pain. More important, whatever fear grips you, your children's terror is magnified. At least *you* have some control over your life; they have none.

- Commit to ensuring that your children have two parents. You gave them that in the beginning. It is their birthright. Remember, too, that however angry you may be at the other parent, this is the parent you chose for them.

- Accept the reality that the process is not going to change the other party. It won't make your spouse more cooperative, less controlling, more financially responsible, honest or a better parent.

- Be realistic. Most of this book is devoted to telling you not what you want to hear, but what *is*. The sooner you get clear that the legal system cannot solve all problems and relieve you of the consequences of decisions you made years ago, you'll accept responsibility for making the best decision you can and be more likely to have a successful divorce.

2

Gold Stars and Magic Wands

Many divorces get off on the wrong track at the beginning because one party either wants credit for having been an exemplary spouse or parent in the past or refuses to accept the reality that a divorce is inevitable. This isn't all a bad dream from which you will awaken in the morning. Divorce, even under the most auspicious circumstances, can be wrenching, traumatic and painful.

If you've been "spouse of the year" for the last 20 years, don't expect a gold star for it. That means nothing to your mate if you've just walked out, whatever the reason. Don't keep looking for validation of all the good you did over the years; it isn't going to be forthcoming, at least not now. Maybe in the hazy future, perhaps when you're dancing at your daughter's wedding or celebrating your first grandchild's birthday, you'll each be able to acknowledge the other, but don't expect it now. And don't give away the store trying to buy validation from your ex. It doesn't work that way.

Similarly, don't check out on the process just because it is painful. You'll have major problems if your attitude toward your divorce is "Wake me when it's over." You probably won't like the decisions which have been made for you during the course of the proceeding. If you elect not to participate, it may be too late to influence the result when you finally decide to pay attention.

The greatest assets you can have at the beginning are a realistic attitude, honest self-examination, and a willingness to learn what you need to know in order to make the best possible decisions under the circumstances.

I have in my office a wand, complete with bells, streamers and gold dust. It was given to me by a client who went through a gut-wrenching two-year divorce after a very long term marriage. She constantly railed against the unfairness of it all. The fairy tale she thought she had been living abruptly turned into a nightmare when her husband left her for a woman who didn't have two brain cells to rub together. She was now going to have to assume financial responsibilities she thought he would handle for the rest of her life and the prospect terrified her. I heard constantly about the failure of her expectations and had great difficulty getting her to look beyond the unfairness she perceived. I would send her to her therapist to deal with her feelings and frequently told her that I wished I had a magic wand which could make it all better, but I didn't. My job, unpleasant as it was, was to tell her the truth, however unpalatable it might be to her, and help her make the best decisions she could under the circumstances. Once she finally got the message, the case settled, and after it was all over, she brought me my own "magic wand." I've used it countless times since, always to make the same point. I'm not in the business of telling you what you want to hear. I'm in the business of telling you the truth and helping you deal with the reality of your legal situation in the healthiest and most responsible manner I can.

So, if you want to do yourself a favor at the beginning, promise to deal with the process as clearly, cleanly and responsibly as you can. Separate dollars from emotions, kids from property, and don't try to rewrite the past. Of *course* you wish things were different. Accept what is, take responsibility for the decisions you made, and actively plan for your future. Don't just drift aimlessly through your divorce. Otherwise, you'll come out on the other end with no clue how you got there.

"But it's not FAIR . . ."

To paraphrase William Goldman's *The Princess Bride,* "Life isn't fair . . . it doesn't have to be." The concept of fairness is utterly subjective. In a divorce, there are as many definitions as there are parents and children. The first awful truth about divorce is that you and your spouse will never agree on what is "fair." You will each feel that you are giving more and getting less than the other. You will probably both be right.

Divorce isn't fair. Don't expect it to be and don't complain because it isn't. Divorce isn't fair because life isn't fair.

The fact is:

A husband who worked 20 years at a job he hates will think it is "unfair" to have to "give" his wife half of his pension while he still has to work at the same lousy job to pay her support.

A wife who gave up her career dreams to move from state to state with her husband's job transfers will think it "unfair" that she is now expected to take her rusty education out into the work place.

That's the way it is.

If you start out with an expectation of "fairness," however you define it, you are doomed to a long and bitter divorce. I don't mean by this that the law is arbitrary, capricious and cruel, even if it sometimes seems to be. It just isn't designed to solve all the problems of a failed relationship. It certainly can't meet every litigant's subjective definition of fairness.

One of the most damaging fallacies which we entertain as Americans is the belief that there is legal redress for every wrong. That simply isn't the case with the legal system in general, and couldn't be more untrue than in family law.

Forgive me for digressing into a little law.

The legal system which we inherited from our forbearers was designed to resolve boundary disputes, criminal guilt and punishment, even patent infringement. It was not designed to decide where children live, who is the better custodial parent or how long one party should receive support from the other. I can think of no issue less suited to the traditional hour's worth of direct and cross examination than child custody. Yet, the vast majority of cases don't even see one hour of court time.

When the legal system addresses those issues, it tries to establish a general rule, a rule that will be equitable (a better term than the endlessly loaded "fair") in more situations than not. There are always some cases which will not fit the rule. Therefore, by definition, there always will be situations in which, given the specific facts, the rule will operate inequitably. That's the way it is. Cases and fact situations slip through the cracks, and there's little that either the lawyers or judges can do about it.

A good example is "pillow talk." Husbands and wives quite literally do not deal with one another at "arm's length," even though the law of contracts usually assumes that they do. They make agreements and promises, all on the assumption that they will always be together. These agreements are rarely reduced to writing, and when the marriage falls apart, memory of the existence of such agreements, much less the content, becomes amazingly selective.

Suppose a husband owns a house where he and the wife and children live. He intends to stay married forever. He says he'll put her name on it, but somehow, in the press of getting the kids to soccer practice, going to work, and the business of day-to-day living, it doesn't get done. So, what happens when somebody decides that "forever" just ended? The law has to make a rule, which means that if it didn't get handled "legally," that wife may very well lose. Whenever there is a general rule, there are going to be individual cases where it works a hardship.

So, why make the rule in the first place? Why not simply let a judge decide each case on its merits? Assuming for a moment that there was money to fund and staff the thousands of courtrooms that would be required to handle the volume of cases (and do you really want to pay the taxes necessary to sustain that many courts?) how could anyone plan and make decisions about his property with any feeling of predictability?

You may find several instances in your own divorce where you think the rule is unfair to you. *Don't* keep going from lawyer to lawyer and judge to judge trying to get someone to tell you what you want to hear. Equally importantly, don't dig in your heels on another issue, trying to get more to "make up" for the fact that the first one went against you. If the law doesn't support your position on the house, don't insist on trying to recoup your "loss" by taking an unreasonable position on support.

Instead, think of "fair" as a four-letter word and lose it from your vocabulary for the duration of your divorce. Instead of looking for what is fair, look for what is practical, what works, what results in maximizing the estate being divided, and what leaves each party with dignity intact.

"I want to be protected . . . "

A corollary to "but it's not fair" is "I want to be protected."

Everyone wants to be protected from the vicissitudes of life, and there are many areas where the law can accommodate you. However, in thousands of other areas neither the law, your lawyer nor the judge can protect you. Remember that life involves risk, and there are countless risks for which there is simply no shelter. That's life.

You may have the best support order in the world. You may have the model ex-husband who not only pays his support on time, he pays it early. Not only does he pay it early, he pays for lots of extras for the kids without being asked and voluntarily agrees to increase the payment from time to time to account for adjustments in his income and the cost of living. What happens when he loses his job, a common event these days? Don't beat your breast and gnash your teeth because the legal system failed you. It didn't. He would have lost his job if you had still been together, and you would have shared the financial hardship with him.

Suppose that instead of losing his job, he's hit by a truck? OK, you say, I'll get lots of life insurance. Suppose, instead of being hit by a truck and dying, he gets hit by a truck and survives? No life insurance will pay your mortgage if he is disabled.

The moral of the story is that there are thousands of contingencies for which protection through the divorce courts is minimal at best. The law can't guarantee the vagaries of the economy, the rising cost of a college education, or traffic accidents. Neither the process, the legal system nor your lawyer can be a guarantor for your future. As with fairness, if you start out with an expectation of protection against every ill wind, you will have a very long, expensive, painful and ultimately bitter divorce and you still won't have the protection you expected.

3

Goals, Strategy
and Tactics

Notwithstanding the proliferation of goal-setting books and workshops, most people don't have a clue what they want out of life. In that case, how can they possibly know what they want out of their divorce? One of the most constructive things you can do at the outset is to get clear about what you want. If *you* don't know what you want, how is your lawyer going to have any chance of getting it for you?

Recognize, too, that there is a vast difference between knowing what you don't want ("I don't want to be married to this jerk") and what you do want ("I want financial independence and a secure home"). Everybody wants the pain to end, but that isn't specific enough to qualify as a goal. Think instead about what you want your life to be like in the future.

I often explain to clients that I don't set your goals; you do. There's a very simple reason for this. Years from now, I'll be off doing something else, and you'll still be living with the consequences of the decisions you make now. If you've failed to set goals for yourself, circumstances will be imposed on you by default and you'll be living with repercussions you never would have consciously chosen.

First, you need to be very clear on what you want, and that it is realistic. You may be quite certain you don't want a divorce. Yet, if your spouse has left and filed for divorce, you don't have much choice, do you? Recognize, too, that what is most important to you at the beginning of a separation may be meaningless a few short weeks or months later as your perspective changes.

Goals need to be set, reviewed frequently, and reset as frequently as circumstances dictate. This is particularly critical at any life-changing juncture such as divorce.

The first thing you should do is to make a list, in no particular order, of everything you would like to see happen in your life. Include both short term and long term goals. Don't try to set priorities yet, and don't worry yet if they don't seem realistic. There's plenty of time to do that later. Just make sure you have an hour or two of uninterrupted time and allow your mind to free-float, writing down everything you think of that you would like to see happen. Don't edit or judge yet. Later you'll have lots of time to delete references to seeing your spouse in cement shoes on a high bridge.

After you've made your list, prioritize it. Look at it frequently. Revise it from time to time as appropriate. Trust me. Your priorities will change with the passage of time. This is particularly important at the beginning. What seems most imperative in the days immediately following separation may well become insignificant with the passage of time. For that reason, I counsel clients not to make any decisions they don't have to for at least three months. If circumstances demand action, that's fine. Make the best decision you can with the facts available to you at the time, but don't go looking for decisions to make. In the days after separation, you may not be able to stand seeing the house you shared together. Before you run out to put it on the market, wait a while for things to jell. It won't seem so empty in a few weeks or months, and it might be the perfect place to be in the years to come.

When making your list, be specific. It's not good enough to simply say your kids are your highest priority. What does that mean to you? Does it mean possession of the kids, keeping them away from the other spouse? If so, the result may be a turf war which will make Bosnia look like a Sunday picnic. Does it instead mean that you want your kids to come through the process feeling as loved and secure as possible? That will lead to an entirely different course of conduct. Decide what you want your kids' and your own lives to be like during and after the divorce. What kind of relationship do you want with your kids? With your ex? Given the realities of your financial situation, where would you like to live? Work? When you look back on your divorce in future years, what do you want to be able to say to yourself?

Always keep your goals in mind. It is far too easy to get consumed by minutia in the day-to-day progress of divorce. If you remain focused on the long range target, you are less likely to be sidetracked by trivia.

I tell clients that I'll spend as much time with them as they need to evaluate the pros and cons, but I don't make the decisions. My role at that point is to steer them toward what I think is realistic and to make sure that they understand the consequences of their choices.

It is important that you understand the difference between goals, strategy and tactics. Clients set goals, the attorney and client set strategy together, and the attorney then develops the tactics to carry out the strategy.

Once goals are set, then it's time to devise a strategy. That's where the client and attorney must be in sync. I'm the one with the knowledge of the process and expertise in the law. Therefore, I'm the one primarily responsible for charting the course, but it must be one with which the client is comfortable.

Your attorney should be able to explain her strategy and why one approach is more likely to be successful than another. Ultimately, if you don't like the course your attorney is taking, you may want to change counsel. However, as long as I'm attorney of record in a case, I insist on being primarily in control of the approach to be used. I'm much more effective if I'm doing things in the way that is most comfortable to me. If my client wants it done another way, I'll probably be less effective and will most likely suggest that he find someone else who is more simpatico with his style.

Strategy needs to be developed at the beginning and periodically revised as circumstances change. This isn't the time to simply let events take their course, or you'll be mired in circumstances and process rather than moving in a positive direction. I was once criticized by another attorney for setting strategy "too early," that is, at the beginning of the case. Excuse me? When else would you plot out how you expect to accomplish your goals? I suppose that explains why he was not particularly successful in his practice.

Finally, we come to tactics. In divorce, I define this as procedure. I get to decide that. If we're going to continue a hearing, or disqualify a particular judge, that's my decision. I'm the one who is responsible for steering your case through the system, and I need to be able to use that system as I see fit and my expertise dictates.

As your divorce progresses, you will find its course much smoother if you can keep this perspective. And, above all, keep your goals in mind. You will be much less likely to find yourself on the courthouse steps wondering how the hell you got there.

4

Recipe for the Divorce from Hell

If you insist on vindication from the courts, you are likely to be disappointed. You will have the "Divorce from Hell." To ensure that happens, just follow this recipe:

- Take a position and staunchly refuse to budge. If your lawyer tells you that even though you may be right on the law, it simply isn't worth the cost of the fight, announce, "It isn't the money, it's the principle."

- Insist that all of your family and friends choose sides. Let them know that if they don't side with you, they're off your list. This will guarantee that your divorce will create the widest possible circle of conflict and generate rifts you'll be regretting for years.

- Insist on litigating every issue. Take the position, "I'm not doing anything unless the judge tells me I have to."

- Don't tell your lawyer the whole truth. Then, when you're caught in the lie, tell a little bit more, but still not all of the truth. This process can be drawn out through several stages until your lawyer will either fire you as a client or you will be left with no credibility whatsoever with the court.

- Engineer an emotional outburst every time there's a four-way settlement meeting or a court appearance. Better yet, remain calm yourself while pushing your spouse's buttons.

- Use each negotiating session as an opportunity to dredge up every instance of marital wrongdoing, real or imagined.

- Define every issue in terms of who "won" and who "lost." I've left the courthouse with a client who got everything she asked for and then wanted reassurance that her husband didn't get anything he wanted. She actually asked me if getting everything we wanted "was a win for us." If it isn't enough for you to get what you want, but instead you have to ensure that the other side didn't get what he wanted, you're in for Armageddon.

- Cling to unreasonable expectations, even after your attorney says they are not realistic. Then, when the judge rules against you (as your attorney told you all along he would) complain accusingly, "we *lost* on everything!" Guess what?. . . It isn't a loss unless there was some possibility of a win.

Part II

Resources

5

Friends, Family and Arm-chair Quarterbacks

It is going to be critical at the beginning to identify the available resources and use each of them appropriately. Some of your most important resources are:

- Therapist

- Lawyer

- Financial advisor

- Friends

- Family

- NEVER the children

If you are far enough along in the process to be drawn to this book, chances are you've already told at least one trusted friend. You are now about to embark on one of the trickiest of friendship issues. Even the "best" of divorces is a traumatic experience. You will need all your resources to get through it. You'll need friends who will just let you vent, and still listen (hopefully with mouths shut). You'll need family to reassure you that you are still loved. Most people have a healthy contingent of both, so what goes wrong?

Well, for starters, some people have a ghoulish fascination for other people's crises. It can stem from a variety of causes. Some of them shudder and think, quite honestly, "There but for the grace of God . . . " Others love to endlessly discuss the problems in your relationship to divert attention from the problems in their own. And, of course, everyone loves a scandal, especially when they know the participants.

Identify your resources and keep them carefully compartmentalized. Don't turn to your friends for legal advice, or your attorney for therapy. If you do, you'll get yourself in serious trouble.

Everyone has a different need for privacy. Some people like to discuss their most intimate business with the bagger at the check-out line. Others don't even tell their co-workers when they separate. Whatever your privacy threshold, at least one good, trusted friend is a godsend. A trusted friend who listens sympathetically and gives no advice is a pearl beyond price.

Suppose your friend, although well meaning, can't refrain from telling you how to proceed. Here are a few of the things you are likely to hear:

"I'd never let anyone treat me that way!"

The implication is that you are being a chump if you don't follow your friend's advice. The problem with this analysis is that no one else is inside your skin. Your friend, however sincere, has absolutely no idea how he would react to that situation until he has had to face it himself. I can't count the times a client has sat in my office, considering whether to stay with a spouse who is having an affair and confessed that for years she's boldly advised her friends, *"I'd* never take him back . . . " You never really know unless it is *your* "him."

"My neighbor/cousin/sister in law/ got everything"; or

"My cousin was left with only the clothes on his back, while his wife got the house, the club membership, and everything else."

Rarely are court decisions or settlements so grossly one-sided. One party may get the bulk of the property, but also all of the debt, which nets out to the same minimal value as the property awarded to the other side. Also, people like to brag/complain about how much/little they got. Stories about the fish that got away are nothing to tales of divorce woe. Frequently, the person repeating the story has no idea of the specific settlement terms. It's hearsay, and they only know as much as they were told. Your source probably has few, if any, of the actual facts, and chances are the cousin's spouse feels exactly the same way.

"Your wife spends a fortune on clothes; you'd better cut off the credit cards before she runs them up."

If there is any hope for retaining relatively good feelings through the course of your divorce, I guarantee that those good feelings will be permanently squelched if you secretly cancel the credit cards and your wife is embarrassed by having the card rejected by her favorite clerk at the local boutique. I know your friend was well intentioned. However, your friend is not going to be the one living with the consequences of the resulting distrust and humiliation. This is a perfect example of the type of "defensive" action that is inevitably viewed as hostile by the other party. (See more detailed analysis in Chapter 33, "The Paranoia Factor.") If you're going to follow your friend's advice, at least be sure you're prepared to accept the consequences. You'll have to. Your friend won't.

"You'd better start hiding money so you have a nest egg."

Again, this is very easy advice to give and almost inevitably backfires. It's relatively easy to hide small sums of cash and, frankly, quite difficult to hide large ones. I frequently tell my clients that if someone has seriously been working for years to hide money, we'll never find it all. However, in my experience, *some* almost always turns up. This means that if you have, again for "defensive" purposes, decided to build your little nest egg, the chances are quite good that it is going to be discovered. When it is, trust and cooperation will die, never to be exhumed, and you won't have much credibility with the judge, either.

Now, I'm not suggesting that you should leave your finances in the control of your soon-to-be-ex. Quite the contrary. One of the most important steps anyone must take is to assume responsibility for his own financial knowledge and well-being. If you have not historically been responsible for handling the family finances, there's no excuse for not educating yourself now. However, actively hiding cash, assets or anything else (and I include hiding pertinent documents) is going to hurt you in the long run.

Suppose someone is crying in his beer to you about being "taken to the cleaners." Consider the possibility that he's deliberately lying. Now, why would he do that, you ask? Perhaps he doesn't want the other side to realize they blew it. Perhaps his attorney did such a good job that the person who thinks he won hasn't any idea how much he actually gave up. I have admonished clients for whom I negotiated particularly good settlements to keep their mouths shut about the fact that the other side overlooked a major weakness in our case. It's just good negotiating to let your opponent think he won, and it's stupid to blow that by bragging on the golf course or around the pool at the country club. That kind of thing *always* gets back through the grapevine.

One final caveat regarding the trusted friend. Your friend probably has a spouse or special someone and, though sworn to secrecy, will probably tell your story. Don't be surprised to have your confidences leak out and get back to your soon-to-be ex.

6

How to Select
a Therapist

I recommend that every client see a therapist. Now, I'm not suggesting six years of psychoanalysis four days a week. However, under the best of circumstances, divorce is an emotionally charged, traumatic experience. Unless nipped in the bud, emotional issues continually bleed through into property, financial, and kid disputes. Even if you are the one who wants the divorce and consider the day you finally had the courage to take the step the best and most liberating of your life, you are still going to hit rough spots. That is simply part of the program. There are going to be times when you second-guess what you have done, why you have done it, and whether there was a better way. I recommend individual counseling at the beginning of every separation and couples counseling for every case in which the parties believe there is even a minute chance of reconciliation. After all, what is the worst thing that can happen? If it doesn't work, and the marriage can't be saved, you find yourself exactly where you were, but with a better understanding of what got you there. And, if divorce is inevitable, your therapist will help you immeasurably in getting through the process. Moreover, a good therapist will help you understand what caused the break up of the marriage, including your role in it, and help you avoid making the same mistake with a clone of your soon-to-be ex a few years from now.

So, how do you select a therapist? Among the best referral sources are other professionals: your own attorney, doctor, minister, children's doctor, teachers, etc. They are likely to know who's well regarded in the therapeutic community. Your attorney will also know a little bit about you, your personality and the case and be able to steer you to one or two therapists who are likely to be a good match. Your friends may also be able to give you referrals. Any consumer of therapeutic services should be able to give you useful advice. You may want to talk with two or three therapists before selecting one to work with.

After the first meeting or two, you will get a sense of whether or not you are connecting with your therapist. It may be that all you need is a couple of sessions to make sure you are on the right track individually and, equally importantly, that you have someone available as a resource when you hit those inevitable rocky spots.

How can you tell if you have a good match with your therapist?

In the first place, a good therapist will give you a very safe place to address your own conflicts and feelings. When you are ready, a good therapist will help you deal with your own role in the marital break up. At the risk of repeating myself, it always takes two. Your therapist can help you extract the lessons to be learned from the experience so that you don't repeat them later on and help you to adopt a constructive and realistic attitude toward the process, your ex and your children. In fact, a good therapist is an invaluable resource in helping you deal with your children and assist them through their own crises.

Find a therapist who's willing to *work* with you. I say this advisedly. Therapy is hard work. If you're not willing to face painful issues, deal with them and resolve them, don't waste your money. Avoid what I call a "cheerleader" therapist. This is someone about whom a patient says, "I really feel great for a couple of hours after I leave her office and then I get just as depressed as ever." This is the kind of therapist who (therapeutically speaking) thumps you on the back and says, "You'll be great." In the long run, this doesn't cut it. Therapy is work, not cheerleading, for both of you. The only lasting value is in increasing self-knowledge, not an artificial shot of adrenalin.

The other thing a good therapist will do is to keep your legal fees down and help you refrain from poisoning your friendships as a result of using either your lawyer or your friends as outlets for the inevitable venting.

Many mental health professionals offer sliding fee scales. If you cannot afford a therapist, look into mental health groups who might offer free or low cost services.

If you can't afford a personal therapist, get into a support group where the cost is shared among several patients. It's not the same as individual therapy, but it can be very useful. Most churches and community centers offer support groups, and you can usually find one in your area. A support group can help immensely by demonstrating that you are not alone, thereby alleviating your sense of isolation. It also can provide a range of practical suggestions for coping with specific situations. Don't ever underestimate the importance of having a group of listeners who can sympathetically point out to you the ways in which you are messing up.

Also, don't overlook the possibility that a support group may benefit your children. Many communities and organizations now offer support groups for children of divorce. In northern California, Kid's Turn does a marvelous job at providing services to kids caught in the divorce of their parents. Check to see if similar organizations or programs exist in your local area. Call your community center, church, or social services organization. Such resources may even be available through the schools.

At the beginning of a divorce, I frequently tell prospective clients that a good therapist is more important than a lawyer. It's more important to be clear about where you are now and how you got there than to start taking legal action. A good therapist can be the best friend you'll ever hire.

7

How to Select
a Lawyer

One of the most difficult and critical decisions you'll have to make is the selection of a lawyer. You'll need to do a lot of homework in order to make a good choice.

First, ask around. Find out who is reputed to be a good *family* lawyer in your area. When someone's name is mentioned, ask why. Decide if the reasons given are consistent with your goals for your divorce. If you're told "She's really nice," and you expect litigation from hell, keep looking. She may be easy to talk to, but get steam-rollered in court. While you want to have good communication with your attorney, you're not interviewing for best friend. You want someone who can do the job. Don't go to an attorney who does not specialize in family law except to get a referral to someone who does. In most jurisdictions, family law is extremely specialized. It takes years to learn to do it well. Someone who just dabbles in it or takes a custody case now and then when cash flow is down is not a good choice.

One of the best sources is other, non-family lawyers. They're familiar enough with the legal system to know who is respected by the insiders. This is always a good place to start.

Ask your friends and neighbors. Find out who represented them, and how they felt about their representation. If they interviewed and rejected other attorneys, find out who and why. Then decide for yourself. Don't blindly assume you would have made the same decision as your friend.

Ask your therapist if you already have one. They frequently know who is good. They have the additional advantage of knowing you, and are therefore more likely to refer you to someone who will be a good fit.

When you've done your research and have amassed a list of names, call around and interview several. I like to talk to prospective clients on the phone before seeing them. I take only a small number of the cases referred to me. If I talk to the client first, it is usually easy to determine if this is a case in which I'm likely to be interested, and if I seem to have good communication with the client. If not, I make a referral on the spot. I have an extensive referral list and take pleasure in being able to suggest two or three attorneys who I think might fit well with the client and case. I take care to match the client with the attorney rather than simply reading down the list, and I only refer to attorneys whose work I know. By the way, if you are referred on in this way, don't ask "But is he any good?" If I didn't think he was, I wouldn't be giving you his name. I always ask the clients if they were given any other names. If I can validate people to whom they have been referred from several sources, they will feel more comfortable about the individual. If the people mentioned are not high on my list of competent colleagues, I invariably say, "Let me suggest a few more."

This part is critical: interview at least two attorneys. Even among the most competent and specialized, there are wide differences in style, strategy and personality. How will you know this if you only talk to one? Find one who meshes with you.

Don't be overly impressed with the attorneys who push "free initial consultation." Though practices vary widely among geographical areas, I've always been of the opinion that *family* lawyers (as opposed to other specialists) who need to advertise free consultations to get clients in the door either haven't been around very long or have trouble getting business. Either way, I'd be worried as a prospective client. I realize there are other areas of the law, such as personal injury, where free initial consultations are the norm, and there are very good reasons for that. I just don't think those reasons carry over into family law. You may well get precisely what you're paying for.

Should it be a man or a woman? There are very few good reasons to let gender be the deciding factor. If you think a man will be tougher, or a woman will understand better or will be "too nice," you will be making a mistake. Don't ever allow sexual stereotypes to dictate your decision. When I'm asked for a referral only to a woman lawyer, I usually give a lecture on gender bias. I point out that hormones are a stupid reason to select an attorney. What they really need is the best attorney for their case, court and personality. I was brought up short once by a woman who somewhat timidly responded that the first lawyer she consulted (a well known local Lothario) had suggested taking out his fees in trade. I told her I understood her fears based upon that experience. The proper response, however, is not to assume that all male attorneys will do the same. Instead, she should report the first attorney to the bar association and continue her search for the best possible attorney for her case, regardless of gender.

Clients frequently ask me to take cases in a distant county. This is a mistake. It is important to find an attorney who is intimately familiar with your local court and judges. An out-of-town attorney is going to be at a distinct disadvantage. This isn't because the local guy can get special favors from the judge. He will, however, be much more familiar with the local rules and may have helped write them. Many areas of family law are highly discretionary, and the local attorney will be more likely to know how a particular judge exercises his discretion. He should know how the judge tends to rule on similar facts and what approach works best with her. He probably knows your opposing counsel, which can work very much in your favor. For these reasons, I decided years ago never to venture out of my county; I know that I have a huge advantage against out-of-county counsel and I certainly don't intend to find myself in the reverse position.

If, even after considering all this, you insist on Ms. Hot Shot Big City Lawyer who doesn't really know your local court that well, consider this: Do you really want to pay her several hundred dollars per hour to drive from her office to the courthouse and back for each hearing, or to research the local rules that the local attorney knows by heart? Think of the advantage the other side will have if they know that each hearing costs you twice as much because of the built-in travel expense. Do you suspect that the extra expense might be used by the other party as a tactic to drive your fees up and force you to settle? You bet.

Many states have certification processes which help you in locating an experienced family law attorney. This is one of many factors to consider, but is not by any means determinative. I'm a certified family law specialist in California, but know many highly competent professionals who are not, not because they couldn't pass the test, but because they didn't bother trying. I also know several certified specialists whom I consider to be idiots. It's one of several questions to ask, but don't reject the attorney who is knowledgeable, highly respected in the legal community, and with whom you happen to have good rapport just because he's not certified. Experience and familiarity with the local family court are infinitely more important.

What other questions should you ask? I'm always amused when a prospective new client comes in with a laundry list of questions obviously culled from a "how to" book. They'll want to know how long I've been in practice (as though 18 years is better than 15), where I went to law school (unless it's Harvard, they generally won't know the difference between a fine local institution and ABC Law School by Mail), or what my "win/loss" record is (more about this later). These questions are not going to elicit any useful information in the search for a divorce lawyer. Unless the ink is barely dry on the diploma, the date of admission to the bar is of significantly less relevance than the quality of experience in your kind of case.

What you want to know is how long they've been doing *family* law, in this locality. What percentage of their practice consists of cases like yours? If it's just something they do when receipts are down and they're having a slow month, keep walking. Ask what they know about the local family judges. What are the procedures? Does the judge have any known biases? How much time are you likely to get with the judge? What does the attorney they think the chances are of settling your case? How much custody work do they do? What are the special problems presented by your fact situation? What is their experience with complex business valuation, or commercial real estate holdings, or stock options, or whatever specific assets you and your spouse will have to divide? Do they think it will be necessary to retain a forensic accountant, that is, one who testifies in court? Why? On what issues? What do they estimate the cost is likely to be? Whom would they recommend, and why? Ditto for custody or visitation evaluators.

It is important that your case is neither the largest they have handled nor the smallest in their office. If it is significantly larger than their other cases, they may not have either the expertise nor the time to handle it properly. If it is the smallest, they may lose interest in it or it may be lost among the others. Either way, you are better off if your case is of a type routinely handled by your prospective attorney.

When you get deeper into the facts of your case, your prospective attorney should be able to tell you her likely strategy and why she thinks it would be more successful or cost-effective than another approach. She should be able to tell you her approach to procedure, and how she likes to run her cases. As professionals, we all have our own styles and should be able to characterize them for the client. I can give a prospective client an excellent rundown on my style, strengths and, yes, weaknesses in about five minutes. If your lawyer doesn't volunteer this information, ask the question. It's a perfectly fair one.

Finally, your attorney should be able to give you a clear understanding of her billing practices and procedures. Almost all family law cases are billed hourly, rather than on a flat fee. You need to know how your attorney structures her billing, what she bills for, whether she bills for paralegal time (most do) and what requirements she has for retainers. How is the retainer held, and how often are you billed? What does she expect from you when the retainer is consumed?

If you already know whom your spouse has retained, your attorney will probably be able to give you a better ballpark estimate on total fees (see Chapter 12, "The Lawyer from Hell"). Remember that since fees are billed hourly, it is virtually impossible to do more than estimate fees generally at the beginning of a case. It is going to be up to you to keep tabs on fees as they are incurred. More about this later, too. (See Chapter 40, "Keeping a Rein on Fees and Costs.")

When you are deciding whether you can afford a particular attorney, assume that you are going to be paying all of the fees, either from the marital estate or individually. I have explained to countless clients that, although we routinely ask that the other side be ordered to pay our fees, they must assume that everyone pays his own. I've even explained the rationale, which is that as a matter of policy, most courts don't like to send litigants the message they can litigate at will for free. It tends to lessen the likelihood of protracted and unnecessary litigation if both sides feel they are at risk for the cost. Despite this speech, which I could now give in my sleep, clients still come back later and say "But I thought *he'd* have to pay for it." Listen, and read my lips. Yes, you will have to pay for it. Assume that to be true and factor it into the selection of your attorney. And don't blithely assume that the hourly rate doesn't matter because the fees will be paid out of the marital estate.

Whose estate is it anyway, and if it is reduced by excessive fees, what makes you think you're not the one paying the freight?

Prospective clients frequently don't understand me when I tell them they don't need someone as expensive as I am for a simple case. Divorce fees are usually hourly. If Attorney Smith charges $300 an hour and Attorney Brown only $200, when should you opt for the more expensive attorney? Do a cost/benefit analysis. If your case involves complex issues which I can handle efficiently because I have handled many similar cases in the past, then you are better off paying the higher rate because I will be more effective. You should not pay someone with a lower hourly rate to educate herself in an area of the law which is new to her. The initial rate will be lower, but the total bill may be much higher because the education will be on the client's dime.

By the same token, if the issues are such that no specialized expertise is required, why should you pay the higher hourly rate when there is no savings in time or result? If the issue is simple and your attorney will just be waiting around the courthouse for a hearing to be called, why not choose the lower hourly rate? I frequently tell prospective clients that they need a competent family law attorney, but that the complexity of their issues is not such that I can handle the case any more efficiently than the next guy. In that instance, there is no benefit to the client (except ego or perhaps scare value) in retaining the Big Gun. It is a good use neither of their money nor of the attorney's time.

Sometimes, all logic to the contrary, a client insists on retaining a more expensive attorney than he needs. I have frequently been in the position of explaining to a client why he really doesn't need me for the facts of his case. I tell him he will be paying far too high a percentage of his net worth for my fees, and there are many other attorneys who are perfectly well qualified to handle the case at a lower hourly rate. Sometimes one insists, "but I want the *best*." Whenever I give in and take a case I know doesn't justify my involvement, I invariably regret it. At some point, the client will realize I was telling the truth and start to resent the hourly rate she agreed to pay. So, you ask, why don't I take the case and just charge the lower hourly rate? Most really good family lawyers have more prospective cases than they can possibly take. If they turn down one case, it is not as though their caseload won't remain full. Believe me, if your attorney tells you that you can do just as well with someone much less expensive, you are being told the truth.

Once you are well into the initial interview, check the quality of your communication. Are you getting straight answers to the questions you are asking? Do they make sense? Do you feel the lawyer is hearing you when you describe your goals and fears? This is a critical issue. The primary cause of a breakdown in the attorney/client relationship is lack of good communication. It is a truism that the relationship never gets better than it was at the beginning. If you are not communicating effectively then, if either of you is having to repeat and explain things to be sure the other understands what you are trying to say, it isn't a good fit. I'll refer clients out without hesitation at this stage if I don't think the communication is satisfactory. I know from past experience that we can't work effectively as a team if we're not on the same wave length, and it will not be a successful professional relationship. I'll also explain to the client precisely why I'm declining the case. Sometimes attorneys take the easy way out. They don't want the client to feel rejected, so instead of telling the truth, they tell a white lie. They quote a fee the client can't afford or say they are suddenly "too busy" to take your case. I've never understood this last one. If they were too busy, why didn't they know that before meeting with you and wasting everyone's time?

Instead, they should be telling you the truth, which is that they don't want your case. It is important to be completely honest here. You and the attorney each have a right to decline a professional relationship. Sometimes clients are surprised to learn this, but, after all, it isn't indentured servitude. If I don't think we have good communication, I say so. That doesn't mean that I don't like you or that you're too stupid to understand what I'm saying. I try to keep it from sounding like a rejection. Instead, I explain what I've just said here. In order for our relationship to be effective in achieving your goals, we have to work as a team. That means our communication must be exemplary and we must agree on the goals and strategy to be employed. If either of those factors is absent, it doesn't mean that one of us is bad or wrong. It just means that it won't work and you should keep on looking.

Remember also that what we do as attorneys is confidential. I can't give you a referral list of satisfied clients or explain just *how* I pulled off a major coup in the Jones case last month. If Mr. Jones himself told you what a terrific job I did and that's why you're here, that's great. But don't ask, and don't expect me to comment if you do.

And if I refer you to another attorney because I don't think we have good rapport, or for whatever reason, don't ask "Is she as good as you are?". . . of *course* not. If I didn't think my way was better than hers, I'd be doing it *her* way instead of mine.

Six Questions Not to Ask Your Prospective Lawyer:

"Are you really tough?"

("No, I routinely surrender at the slightest hint of opposition . . . ")

I'm always baffled by the frequency with which I get this question. What do they think I'll say? "Not really, but my assertiveness trainer says I need to practice in adversarial situations so I'll get better at it . . . " If you've done your homework and investigated who has a good reputation in your area, you must assume that there's a reason this attorney is well respected. Don't ask this, but instead, ask the questions I suggested earlier. After all, even if your prospective attorney is the wuss of the Western World, either he thinks he's a tough guy (roar) or he knows he's a pussycat but is hardly going to admit it to you. Interestingly, the same client who wants to be sure I'm truly a "barracuda" (a word used only by laymen and never by lawyers) will frequently turn around and tie my hands, not wanting me to do anything that will "make my husband mad."

Corollary: *"I hope you take this as a compliment: I hear you're a real shark"*

I don't and it isn't. If you think being very, very good at what I do is synonymous with being a shark, I don't want you. Sooner or later you'll ask me to do something I consider unethical (but any "shark" would do) and we'll have a parting of the ways. I'll be insulted and you will think I wasn't "aggressive" enough.

"What is your win/loss record?"

This is a meaningless question in a family law context. Divorce isn't like criminal law where you can quantify convictions per number of trials.

How do you even define a win? I might consider it a huge victory to take a terrible case on dreadful facts and turn it into a 50/50.

Suppose there were five issues in my last trial, and I managed to win on the three about which felt strongest. Is that a win? What if those other two issues were the ones in which the other party was most invested? Did he think he won, too? Does that mean I didn't?

"What is your track record against Attorney X?"

This question is almost as meaningless as the last. Instead, ask if your attorney has a history against Attorney X. What happened? Did the case(s) settle? Is there a left over dispute between the attorneys that will affect your case? Was there a mutual effort to resolve the conflict as quickly and amicably as possible, or was the case pushed to its litigious limits? If so, what would your prospective attorney suggest as a strategy against Attorney X in your case?

"Can my husband bribe the judge?"

At the risk of sounding naive to those of you who have been

watching too many old movies, the days of judges being purchased are about gone. Most judges are underpaid, hard-working and sincere individuals who honestly do their best to dispense justice as even-handedly as possible. For those few who are not, there are judicial watchdog commissions which are becoming ever more vigilant. The fact is, even if the judge were amenable to bribery, the risks are simply too great to take a chance. Besides, your spouse couldn't come up with enough cash to make it worth his while. Though judges are undoubtedly underpaid, only an incredibly stupid one would risk the public and professional humiliation, not to mention criminal sanctions, which would result.

"You're a woman, so won't you side with my wife?"

Besides being sexist, this is also stupid and insulting. It assumes that your prospective attorney is so unprofessional as to be guided solely by hormones. After a few well-chosen words on my part, the prospective client who asks me this question either sheepishly apologizes or leaves to find a rough, tough, shoot-em-up gunslinger more to his liking.

Corollary: "*I know you'll understand (agree with me) because you're a woman.*"

When a new client says this to me, I always try (with limited success) to bite my tongue. This isn't sisterhood; it's business. I find the implication offensive and rarely agree to represent a client who starts out this way. If I decide to work with you, it will be because you have a case that interests me and not because we both have ovaries.

"My husband is SO intimidating . . . are you sure you can stand up to him?"

This is a variation on the first comment above and is just as unlikely to elicit any information which will be useful to you in deciding whether you want to retain an attorney. *You* might find your spouse extremely intimidating. Chances are I won't. I wasn't married to him and don't have the emotional baggage that you do.

He may have intimidated you for 20 years. The fact that he doesn't intimidate someone else is not a criticism of you. It is a recognition of the reality that I have no history or connection with him. Surprisingly to many of my clients, I don't care what a tough guy he thinks he is. It's business, and he's on *my* turf.

8

Why You Want Your Spouse to Have a Good Lawyer, Too

The last thing you want when you are starting a divorce is for your spouse to hire a stupid lawyer. More often than not, when I tell my client that the attorney who is going to be representing the other side is a good lawyer, he winces. That's because he doesn't understand the extreme cost which *he* may have to pay for a stupid opponent. He assumes that if the other attorney isn't very good, that means that we win. There are, in fact, times when this happens. I have, on several occasions, obtained an extremely good settlement simply because the other attorney hadn't a clue what he was giving away. It doesn't happen as often as you would think, however. The stupid attorney is easy to beat at court. However, if you really want to settle your case without going to court (and who wouldn't) the stupid attorney will make it much more difficult to do so.

The likely result is that incompetent counsel on the other side of your case will vastly increase the fees, acrimony, and general craziness — all out of proportion to the benefit to you of some issue which he might overlook through ignorance.

Let me explain.

First, we need to define some terms. By "stupid attorney," I mean someone who is incompetent, ignorant, unfamiliar with family law or just plain "doesn't get it." This will distinguish the "stupid attorney" from the "Lawyer from Hell" referred to in Chapter 12. The Lawyer from Hell is someone who very much "gets it." He is generally quite bright, intimately familiar with the ins and outs of the system and manipulates it for his own and sometimes his client's benefit. The stupid attorney is generally acting from very good motives. He just doesn't know any better and can completely wreck a case as a result.

The stupid attorney will be rigid

On some dim level, he knows that there is a great deal he doesn't know. Therefore, he will cling quite rigidly to whatever position he thinks he *does* know. This means that there will be absolutely no creativity in the way his client's case is handled. Because a particular approach worked once for him in another case, he will desperately cling to that same approach, even when it is clearly not working. If your attorney suggests a novel solution which creatively solves the problem, he will be afraid to agree for fear it is a trick or a trap. Since he doesn't have the ability or the experience to think through all of the permutations of the admittedly creative suggestion, he will stick to the "safe," the tried and true. Mind you. He is not doing this out of bad motives. He wants to be sure that his client is protected. He doesn't want to take the risk, and the liability, of making a mistake by recommending something which he doesn't fully understand. Since he knows in his heart of hearts that the other attorney is brighter than he is, he will take the safe way out and say no to the novel solution, in case he missed something. It is extremely difficult to settle a simple case with an attorney such as this. The elegant solution to a complex problem is totally impossible.

A stupid attorney will be unrealistic

Because she is stupid, she will be blind to the weaknesses of her own case. This means she won't see the fact that she really can't win on a particular issue because the facts or the law are against her. One of the hallmarks of a good lawyer is to remain objective with respect to her case so that she can spot not only the strengths but the weaknesses. If the weaknesses can't be turned into strengths or compromised in some way, they should be conceded. One of the worst disservices an attorney can do for a client is to continue to fight even in good, though misguided faith, on a losing issue. All this does is increase the legal fees and animosity. Some of the worst attorneys I know are in fact very bright individuals. However, they have blind spots to the weaknesses of their case and as a result, we litigate *everything*. You don't want an attorney like this, nor do you want your spouse to have one.

I have literally pleaded with opposing counsel to simply read a particular code section which absolutely demonstrated that his position could not possibly prevail under the law. He was a real estate attorney who decided to branch out into family law because the divorcing couple owned lots and lots of real estate. He assumed because he knew about real estate law he knew how to handle real estate in a divorce. Wrong. The only response I got to that letter (which in fact included a copy of the code section which said that he was dead in the water) was a sarcastic reply demanding to know who appointed me Goddess of Family Law. Before we finally got to trial on the issue he couldn't win, $100,000 in attorneys' fees had been consumed. Now, mind you, my client ultimately won about $150,000 on that issue. However I can assure you that he would have gladly compromised it at the beginning, and in fact offered to do so, because he would have preferred to see his ex-wife have the money than pay it to the attorneys. The wife's attorney couldn't see it and his client missed out on a very good deal.

A stupid attorney will get emotionally involved in the case

I have said before that one of the most important attributes of a good divorce attorney is objectivity. This enables her to see the weaknesses in your case and prevents her from being blinded to reasonable settlement opportunities and creative solutions. When an attorney becomes emotionally invested in the case and decides to become a "savior" for her client, she is at risk of becoming a co-dependent. Trust me. This does not help.

We all know that emotions run high in divorces. The client will call his attorney, absolutely outraged at some conduct by the other party and demand that a "strong letter" be sent to the other side. I am not a fan of the "he said/she said" form of correspondence. It serves no purpose other than to momentarily gratify the sender's client and utterly inflame the other party. Some attorneys have turned this into an art form. A bad attorney will literally paper you with these letters (all of which cost money, of course) simply because the client insists on them. The better attorney is the one who refuses to write them unless they serve a useful purpose. I can assure you that the likelihood of settlement decreases significantly once such an exchange is started.

A stupid attorney will create unrealistic expectations

Since by definition a stupid attorney does not know the law, either through ignorance or simple inability to understand it, the information he gives your spouse may in fact be incorrect. This will create unrealistic expectations. He may lead your spouse to believe that he can't possibly lose an issue which hasn't been won in your state since 1912. How likely do you think it is that your spouse will settle if that is what he has been told?

Let me give you an example. Let's suppose that you and your spouse have a family business. Let's suppose that he runs it. For pur-poses of this example, it doesn't matter whether he is a computer consultant, doctor, lawyer, dentist or consulting engineer. He has a business which depends almost entirely on his personal expertise for its value. In a community property state, that business is likely to be deemed to have some sort of "goodwill," that is, an intangible value for which you, as the nonemployee spouse, are entitled to be compensated.

This has happened to me dozens of times. The owner of the business comes into my office, and when I start talking about valuing the business for the property division, he says:

"It doesn't have any value because I can't sell it"; or

"It doesn't have any value because it is worthless without me and I'll just quit."

When I point out the facts of life, he says "You mean I have to buy her out of the business because it is going to make money in the future, and then I have to *pay her* support from those future earnings?"

Precisely.

Now a good attorney will allow the client to vent and then explain the law. It may not feel good and it may not feel fair, but that's the way it is, at least in my jurisdiction.

If that same person goes to a stupid attorney, the stupid attorney may well tell him that he is right. "We're going to take the position at court that since you can't sell this business, it has no value," or, "We are going to take the position at court that since it depends solely on your personal skills, contacts and referral base, it has no value." Now, mind you, the Attorney from Hell may tell the client the same thing, but for different reasons. He knows better but this is a way to make sure that there is a fight which is going to generate lots of fees. The stupid attorney doesn't and will create World War III out of sheer ignorance. You don't want this.

In the fact pattern outlined above, how likely do you think it is that the parties are going to be able to reach agreement on the value of that business?

So, what can you do about it?

If you find that your attorney's theory of the case is radically different from the opposing attorney's theory of the case, pay attention. If your attorney is telling you that it is "the law," and the other side is getting the opposite advice, one of them is wrong. Either it isn't "the law" or one of them doesn't know the law. This is a good time to get a second opinion and find out which attorney is operating under the proper theory. In all but a few unusual "leading edge" fact patterns, there is in fact a body of law, and an experienced attorney will be able to give you some general parameters of what to expect. If you are the one who is getting bad advice, this is a good time to change attorneys. At least you have control over that situation.

If you find your spouse is getting the bad advice, you have a problem. You have *no control* whatsoever. If you tell him that his lawyer is stupid, he will assume the reason you want him to change lawyers is because you are intimidated by the one he has. This will be counterproductive. You may never be able to persuade your spouse to get a second opinion. This is why you want him to start out with a good lawyer in the beginning. Two good lawyers will know the law as it applies to facts such as yours. They will also know where the gray areas are and can very quickly hone in on those rather than spending lots of time and money fighting over routine issues. Those fights can cost you and your spouse tens of thousands of dollars.

Why not simply let your spouse go off happily misguided in a fog of unrealistic expectations?

First, in virtually every case, reaching an agreement (i.e., settling) is preferable to going to trial. It is cheaper, faster, and preserves more dignity for both of you.

Second, if your spouse's attorney is spending tens of thousands of dollars scheduling depositions and doing all sorts of ridiculous things to try to prove the unprovable, your attorney also has to attend those depositions and review the documents and all of the rest of it. That costs *you* money.

Incidentally, even the greatest civil or criminal litigator can fall into the category of "stupid attorney" as described in this chapter if he doesn't have extensive family law experience and is foolish enough to think he doesn't need it.

Clients sometimes ask me to give them a list of attorneys to give to their spouse at the beginning of the case. I used to refuse to do this on the theory that the spouse was going to assume it was a setup and I was giving them somebody who would roll over and play dead at the first opportunity. However, after a few run-ins with really stupid attorneys, I changed my mind. If asked, I now will give a list of attorneys, and they will all be good ones. They will be the people who are very knowledgeable in family law, familiar with our local courts and judges. They will be people I know have a track record of doing a good job for their clients in similar cases and who can find reasonable solutions to difficult problems. The opposing client may or may not select anybody on my referral list, but at least I know that I have done my part to avoid the divorce from hell.

9

How to Tell if You Are Well Represented

Whenever you venture into unfamiliar legal waters, one of the hardest things you'll have to do is evaluate whether you are getting good professional advice. This is particularly true in family law. You may not know much about dentistry, but if you have a bad dentist, the filling will fall out or your tooth will start hurting. But what if you have a bad lawyer?

This is particularly difficult in family law because no one wins everything. Further, you may *both* feel like you're losing the preliminary skirmishes. Every so often I hear through the grapevine that someone whom I (and the rest of the local family law bar) know to be a flaming idiot is touted as God's gift to the legal profession. I can only assume that the source of the referral is either someone who didn't realize what good representation was, or whose case was such a fluke that even a buffoon couldn't screw it up. When I'm asked about such a person, I'll generally say something like "let me give you some more names . . ." and refer them to several people whom I know to be good.

You can't assume that your lawyer screwed up because you "lost" the first hearing (and I remind you that in family law, "lost" is a relative term). I'm a fan of planning for the long haul. If a few concessions need to be made along the way, I don't lose a great deal of sleep if we're still on track for the major goals.

So, what *should* you look for?

First, your attorney should be willing to explain his strategy to you. He should be able to tell you why, in his opinion, a particular strategy is more likely to succeed in your case than another. He should have some experience with similar situations and the same judge to draw upon. He should have a sense of how this judge is likely to respond to your factual and legal situation. After all, one of the criteria you used in selecting him in the first place was his familiarity with the specific court and cases similar to yours.

He should be able and willing to look you in the eye and tell you bad news. We would all prefer to be the bearers of only good tidings. That doesn't often fall to our lot as lawyers. One of the hallmarks of bad lawyering is to fail to be honest with the client about the risks of his case. I've sat on many a courthouse bench listening to the attorney next to me explain the law to his client, only to have him waffle on the hard answer when the client asks, "Does this mean we're going to lose?" A good attorney can and must look you in the eye and answer that question truthfully so you can make realistic decisions about conceding a position you can't win, or trading it for something else you want in a negotiated settlement.

Your attorney should be able to explain your options to you, as well as the advantages and disadvantages of the probable result from each. I've separately discussed the issue of goal-setting. You, the client, have the right and the responsibility to set your own goals, consistent with the law and your (and your attorney's) ethics. In order to do this, you may need to take a considerable amount of time to be sure you fully understand the options available to you, what is realistic and what is not, the possible consequences, approximate cost of each and probability of success. This doesn't mean your attorney can guarantee an outcome. However, he should be able to assist you in properly evaluating the choices available to you.

If you have any doubts, get a second opinion. I give second opinions all the time, as do most family law attorneys. I'm happy to review a file and tell the client what I think. Sometimes I find I would have handled it differently, but that both strategies are judgment calls. In that instance, I would generally defer to the attorney who has had the case from the beginning and knows more about its strengths and weaknesses than I could probably determine in an hour's consultation. Although I may have approached certain issues differently, I find no particular fault. Invariably in those situations, I give clients a list of questions to ask and send them back to their own attorney to get the answers. I suspect that in those cases, the problem is not that the attorney is mishandling the case, but rather that he is not involving the client. Frequently this is as simple as not bothering to explain to the client why Course A is better than Course B or, more likely, not returning phone calls. I happen to be a fanatic about returning phone calls, but many people aren't. I would explain that to the client and send him back to ask the attorney to explain the reason for the strategy. More often than not there's a reasonable explanation which simply hasn't been communicated effectively to the client.

There is a caveat attendant to this: Have you, as the client, provided a clear and accurate recitation of the facts to your attorney? Many people don't. You may leave something out, assuming it "isn't important" or, more frequently, out of embarrassment. Make sure you have given your attorney the complete, unvarnished truth, even if you wish some of it had happened differently, before you start complaining about the course the case is taking.

When giving a second opinion, I would also not hesitate to tell the client if I think he's being badly represented. This doesn't mean just that I would have done something else; everyone has a different style. However, if I don't think the first attorney is maximizing the strong points of the case or properly evaluating the weak ones, the client needs to know that.

If your attorney constantly makes excuses to you for bad rulings, take a close look. We've all been in situations where the judge does something unaccountable. They have great discretion in many areas, and they're human, too. They bring their own baggage of experiences to the bench and sometimes they blow it; that can happen to anyone. But if it happens every time, there's something wrong. If the judge has a track record on cases such as yours, your attorney should know about it. If the judge is truly a loose cannon, why didn't he warn you to stay out of court and try to settle at the beginning? These are legitimate questions.

The second opinion can be invaluable. It may send you back to the first attorney with a new appreciation of what is involved in your representation. It may, on the other hand, result in your changing representation. Either way, the cost of the consultation is money well spent.

10

Attorney/Client Relations

("I thought you were on my side ... ")

At some time during your divorce, you may start to lose faith in your attorney. Maybe you don't understand why a particular strategy is being adopted. Perhaps you feel you and your attorney are not on the same wave length anymore. In my experience, 90% of the problems that arise in attorney/client relations result from poor communication.

Most attorneys are paid on an hourly basis. This means that time is money and, as a result, all too many attorneys take on more cases than they can comfortably handle. Some phone calls may not get returned as quickly as one would like. I'm not defending it, but simply describing a common situation.

Very few family lawyers make a great deal of money. Family law is notoriously one of the least lucrative areas of law. A very simple fact accounts for this: our clients generally can't write off our fees on their tax returns. Businesses can afford to pay much higher legal fees because, of course, Uncle Sam subsidizes a large percentage of those fees by making them tax deductible. Divorce attorneys' fees are generally after tax, after mortgage, after child support and after utilities. This means that many divorce attorneys take on more cases than they can comfortably handle because they know they may be carrying accounts receivable for a long time. It may take months or sometimes years to be paid for the work they are doing today. They accept more cases, because the staff and rent still have to be paid in the interim, while they are waiting for a house to sell or the IRA to be liquidated or some other source of payment. This is not an excuse for not returning phone calls, but it is an explanation of why some attorneys feel compelled to overextend for economic reasons.

This does *not* mean that your case should be ignored, that it should not be given full attention, and that your phone calls should not be returned. That is your right as a client and you should insist on it.

There is a corollary here, as well. If you are constantly calling your attorney and screaming at him because of some unrealistic expectation, such as he can't make your spouse become someone other than the person he's been since the dawn of time (that is, before you even married him), don't be surprised that he is not overly anxious to return the call and get screamed at yet again.

If you feel your attorney is not communicating with you, you must insist that she do so. If she doesn't, it may be time to make a change.

Your attorney should be able to explain to you quite succinctly and in layman's terms the following:

- Her strategy for attaining your goal of getting the house (or some other asset) awarded to you;

- Why he thinks Approach A is going to be more likely to be successful with Judge X than Approach B.

- Why, given the dynamics and personalities of your spouse and spouse's attorney, a four-way settlement meeting would (or would not) be likely to be productive.

- If you insist on fighting for your pension, the likely result and cost, including expert witness fees.

- Why Ms. Jones is a better custody evaluator for your case than Dr. Smith.

- Why you are likely to lose on your claim that you invested $50,000 in the landscaping of his mother's house.

The bottom line in all of the above is that it is your divorce and not your attorney's. Your attorney can only assist you to the extent that she understands and supports your goals.

If you are losing confidence in your attorney, pay particular attention to the reasons *why* she says you're not going to win on a particular issue. As someone who has built a practice and a reputation on the ability to look people in the eye and give them the unvarnished truth, I am a great fan of the attorney who can give bad news unflinchingly, even if it means the client is going to be angry. I consider that part of my job. If your attorney tells you that your position is (a) legally right, but (b) not cost-effective, pay very close attention. If your attorney were out to run up your fees, he would like nothing better than to have you spend thousands of dollars to chase a few hundred. When he will tell you instead that even though you are technically right, the cost of winning exceeds the value to be received, he is telling you the truth.

Suppose you're feeling a little uncertain about your attorney's handling of the case. Talk to the attorney, not her secretary, not her paralegal. The person whose expertise and knowledge you need is your attorney's. You have to have absolutely crystal clear communication.

Make sure that part of your dissatisfaction with your attorney is not that he is refusing to be a shrink. It is fair neither to him nor to you. I frequently tell clients I am a first-rate attorney but that doesn't make me even a third-rate therapist. They can get a first-rate therapist for a much lower hourly rate than mine. Don't expect a lawyer to be therapist, or vice versa.

Most family lawyers are truly committed to helping their clients survive what is probably the most traumatic legal matter they will face. We really do want to make it better. Sometimes that desire seduces us into crossing over the line between attorney and therapist. There may be a very needy client who absolutely has to have daily contact, who is constantly dropping into the office not so much to deliver the paperwork, but to have a "fix," reassurance that someone is there who cares, who understands, and who wants to help. Most of us select our staffs with an eye to finding individuals with the ability to exhibit precisely those traits. This does *not* mean that they should be used as therapists.

So, what happens when your attorney looks you in the eye and tells you something you absolutely, positively, in your heart of hearts *do not want to hear?* Well, I frequently get the comment, "But I thought you were on *my* side . . . "

I'm sorry. My job is not to tell you what you want to hear; my job is to tell you the truth. I would much rather be able to tell you that, yes, of course, I can get you precisely what you want at a fraction of the cost we originally estimated. You would go away happy, I would feel satisfied that I had gotten a good result, etc. That ain't the reality.

The point is, I am on your side. If I weren't, I wouldn't tell you the bad news you don't want to hear. I would do the opposite. I would shine you on and let you keep paying me to fight for something I cannot possibly win. I don't; instead I tell you the truth. I don't expect you to say thank you, but it's nice when you do. You should.

Relationships With Opposing Counsel

There is a very natural fear which goes like this:

If you are friends with my spouse's counsel, won't you get together over drinks and cut a deal which is not in my best interests? Will you give away my case in order to preserve your friendship? If my spouse's attorney seems to know the judge better than you, does that mean that he'll get a better ruling?

In all honesty, I have to tell you that there are extremely isolated instances where this occurs. However, in 99.9% of the cases, it is irrelevant.

Many attorneys are acutely aware of these issues. I remember dealing with an attorney with whom I had many cases over the years. I knew her well and yet, whenever we met at court, she insisted on calling me by my last name, as if we were strangers. She would explain to me, *sotto voce*, that she didn't want her client to think we were too familiar.

In any family law court, anyone who has been around for a period of time has had cases against most of the other family lawyers. They may have gone to law school together and will certainly meet at the continuing education seminars we are all required to attend. The top lawyers will have opposed one another countless times over many, many years. This is true for every level of practice. We may, in fact, have a social relationship with one another.

What I am about to tell you now is the truth: If a case is highly adversarial, if it gets out of hand, something is going to have to give. With any good attorney, what is going to give is not the client's interest but the friendship. I have been there too many times to not know this. I have had too many friendships suffer as a result of the fact that both attorneys know that the clients' interests must come first. There have been moments when I have sworn to the heavens that I will never again take a case against a friend because of the personal price that I (and he) have paid. If my colleague and I aren't willing to pay that price, we simply agree not to take cases against each other anymore. There has never been a case to my knowledge where the client has suffered as a result of that relationship. On the other hand, there have been countless cases where I believe the clients on both sides have benefitted from the fact that the attorneys could work together, both had an understanding of a reasonable resolution range and could get to that range early.

Don't be frightened if your attorney says of his opposing counsel "Oh, I know Joe, we've had cases for years." Chances are that is going to help you, not hurt you.

The same is true for judges. I have known many judges very

well over the years. Not once have I felt that it enabled me to gain an unfair advantage over the other attorney or the other party.

Don't get all excited if your prospective attorney is on a first-name basis with the judge. Judges are on a first-name basis with any number of people whom they do not respect as practitioners. What does matter is that your attorney has developed a reputation for credibility within the court and with a particular judge. The judge will know that if the attorney makes a representation it is because he or she believes it to be true. That counts for a great deal. You could be Mother Teresa and if the judge believes your attorney is a liar he will not reject your position out of hand, but it may be a much harder sell.

Here is another fact of life: Attorneys don't get to select which side of the case they are on. That depends on who called us first. Also, we're not perfect and sometimes we hear one side of a story and it sounds quite credible — until we hear the other side. I would like to say that I have always represented the guy in the white hat. It isn't so. There are times when I have misread my client and, in fact, there are times when I have been flat-out lied to. I have tried cases such as these in front of judges whom I know respect me. I can tell by the ruling that I didn't get any favors and, more often than not, justice was served.

So, when you walk into the court for that initial hearing, don't go into a panic because your attorney says to opposing counsel "Joe, I haven't seen you in a while. How are the kids?" Generally family law is a very small club, we know one another and we are quite professional.

Finally, think about it this way. If you are going into a court where everybody knows everybody, do you *really* want to be the only one with an attorney that no one has ever heard of? Let me rephrase it. Do you want to be the only one with an attorney the *judge* has never heard of? I think not.

11

Courts and Judges

You're getting divorced. That means that if you and your mate are not able to settle your differences, a person in a black robe is going to make decisions which will have consequences for the rest of your lives. Before you delegate this power to a stranger, educate yourself on what that really means. Take a long, hard look at the judge who will be deciding your support rights, where your kid lives and what happens to your worldly goods. After doing so, you may want to reconsider that "outrageous" settlement offer your spouse made last week.

Courts come in all shapes and sizes. Some are majestic and imposing, some downright shabby, some hushed and reverential, others crowded and noisy. Some look just like the set of "Perry Mason," and others more closely resemble the "pit" in a commodities market or the local Department of Motor Vehicles. All have certain common characteristics: They are stark, sterile, and quite public. Secrets you wouldn't share with your dearest friend are freely aired in front of total strangers day in and day out. Litigants are frequently surprised to learn about the lack of privacy. I tell them most of the people watching are too terrified about their own upcoming hearings to pay much attention to your problems. That is true, to a point. It also stinks to have to bare your soul in public. No one in his right mind would do so by preference.

Here's another common factor: in this era of reduced government revenue, there is less and less money to fund the court system. With the increasing pressure for more law and order, fewer and fewer of the limited available funds are being diverted to family law courts. Couple that with rising divorce rates and it doesn't take a rocket scientist to tell you there's not enough court time available.

There are many variations between calendars. A calendar refers to how many cases are expected to be heard on a particular day and how much time is allocated to each of them. Most counties have a combination of "short-cause" and "long-cause" court calendars. A short-cause matter is typically limited to 20 minutes and is designed for family law triage: to make quick and dirty decisions about who lives where, what happens to the kids pending a custody evaluation, who gets the use of the car, and how much support gets paid (and by whom) in the interim pending resolution of the rest of your case.

20 minutes? It would be funny if it wasn't true.

Moreover, in a busy county a judge may have as many as 20 to 40 twenty-minute matters on a morning calendar, and I have seen as many as 60. You heard me. Between 9:00 a.m. and noon, up to 40 cases must be heard and disposed of. They can't spill over into the afternoon because starting at 1:30, there is another full calendar to be decided before 5:00 p.m. It doesn't take a Rhodes scholar or mathematician to figure out that it can't be done. And even if each case had the full 20 minutes allotted, what kind of time is that to determine the family income, how the bills are to be apportioned, who is to receive what support and what restraining orders are needed in order to preserve body and mind, pending the resolution? I guarantee you, there is nothing more taxing to judges than to have to make these decisions in what they know is insufficient time on inadequate information. But someone has to make a decision because the parties couldn't work it out themselves, and so the judge is elected.

Suppose you're one of the lucky ones who can afford to wait for a "long-cause" set. Typically, this means one or two hours on the court's calendar. In my county, that will happen one to three months after the initial filing. Assuming that each party has the financial wherewithal to pay the bills during the interim, you may be able to wait that long before the support order goes into effect. Again, think about it: Two hours to decide who lives where, the family income, how much support should be paid, who has custody of the kids, what the visitation schedule could be, etc. Solomon himself couldn't consistently make good decisions under those circumstances.

As a group, family law judges are extremely conscientious and hard working. They sincerely try to do the best they can with the facts before them and are acutely aware of the financial and human cost of a bad decision. There is probably no other area of the law in which the emotional content is so high and the pressure and volume so great. Family law judges have a notoriously high burn out rate. Day in and day out, they must make gut-wrenching decisions in cases where there is frequently no clear right and wrong. They have to do the best they can with the information presented to them, often knowing they lack important data. Nevertheless, even on partial information, a decision must be made, and so it is. But let's look a little closer at that one or two hours of court time.

The American legal system is based upon direct and cross-examination, questions and answers. Thanks to O.J., everyone in the country is intimately familiar with this concept. It may work fine for real estate disputes but, frankly, it's a lousy way to get to the bottom of who's the best custodial parent. It is slow and cumbersome. If you only have an hour, your attorney is probably going to be forced to do one of two things: either he'll have to consume far too much of that hour's time objecting to questions (because even though the questions may be technically improper that is the quickest way to get evidence before the judge), or he's going to simply have to let the objections go and trust the judge's expertise and knowledge to know the difference between hearsay and credible evidence. And *this* is the system that is going to decide your and your kids' future . . . ?

I say this not to frighten you, but to educate you to the reality. Courts are a place of *last* resort. Someone who has to ask the court to decide these things has failed; failed to settle. That tells me that at least one of the parties and/or one of the attorneys is refusing to accept a reasonable solution.

Let's look at it in very practical terms. You've been served a Summons to show up at court at a particular time on a particular day. You walk into the building on a "short-cause" day. This means that from 20 to as many as 60 cases may be pending for that morning. At least two sides will show up on each case, either "pro per" (that is, representing themselves without attorneys) or with attorneys. Between two and four people will be in court for each of these matters that morning. All of them will be milling around the cold marble (or, in some courthouses, fake marble) hallways awaiting their turn. The competent attorneys are desperately trying to settle their cases, or at least settle some of the issues and thereby make the best use of their time before the judge by reducing the number of areas to be covered. As you sit there on your hard bench, the following questions may be running through your mind:

"Will I be able to pay my house payment next month?"

"What if I don't get to see the kids?"

"What if I'm kicked out of the house; where will I go?"

"Will I be able to live on what's left over after the support order is made?"

This is the truth. This is what really happens.

So, what can you do about it?

Anyone contemplating divorce should take a day or two or three and go sit in your local family court. It's well worth the cost of half a day's pay to sit and watch the judge who will be deciding *your* fate. How do you feel about that judge? Was she hurried? Despite the press of cases, did she seem to be listening and hearing what people were saying to her? Was he trying to be fair to both sides? What was his attitude toward the attorneys and the litigants? Did she seem to favor men over women, or vice-versa?

Then watch the attorneys. Who did you think did a good job? Recognize that as with so much else in law, "good job" is a relative term. It isn't the attorney who was able to reduce the opposing client to tears in the shortest possible time. More constructively, it probably is the attorney who was able to get the most relevant information before the judge in the time allotted. If he asks the same question more than once, lose 5 points. Remember, the biggest fault of the system is that there isn't enough time to get sufficient information into the hands of the person who's going to have to make the decision. Recognize, too, that with the press of these calendars, the judge has likely not read the files in advance; it would be simply impossible to do so.

Therefore, the better attorney is the one who can educate the judge about the relevant facts in the shortest available time so that the best possible decisions can be made under these totally absurd conditions.

That's the attorney whose card I would ask for.

Another advantage of hanging around the courthouse is to talk to the litigants. If someone has been ordered to "show cause" at 8:30, the case may not even be called until 11:15. This means that he faithfully showed up at 8:30 (because, of course, the one time he didn't show up at 8:30 was the day his case was first on the calendar). In the interim, he is sitting in the hall, anxiously awaiting his turn. Perhaps his attorney is there with him, but most likely, the attorney is either talking to the opposing counsel trying to settle the case or handling one of a couple of other cases she has going that morning. The experienced litigant will probably pull out a book or magazine, but most people will be tense and fearful, not knowing what to expect.

They are a wealth of information. Strike up a conversation with someone who looks like they might be in your position. Find out how they feel about their own attorney and the opposing attorney.

Ask if they've been through the system before and how many hearings they've had and what happened (if they're willing to tell you). I don't mean you should invade people's privacy. However, the fact is that many litigants are only too glad to talk about the process with strangers they meet at the courthouse. Utilize this as a resource.

If, after doing all of the above, you still don't feel that settling a case is by far the preferable alternative, either you haven't been paying attention or you should review Chapter 4, "Recipe for the Divorce from Hell" and lose 10 karma points.

A final word on judges: I have said before that the vast majority of them are extremely sincere and work very hard to deliver justice under distressing circumstances. But with the best intent in the world, even on a long-cause case, the judge doesn't know who really lives inside your skin or that of your spouse, much less your children's. With any luck, the judge will never see your children because children don't belong in the courtroom. If you come into court litigating five issues, the judge has no way of knowing that if you could only win on three of them, it would be numbers two, four and five, and you would gladly concede numbers one and three. Why doesn't the judge know that? Because if you told the judge, that's precisely what would happen and you'd never have a chance at the other two. If you are going to do that, you might as well have conceded them at the beginning.

Even if the judge has read your file, in fact, *studied* your file before your case was called, that file is not going to tell him that Johnny can't stand to sleep with the light out or that Matthew gets stomach aches at any disruption in his schedule or that if there isn't enough money for ballet lessons, Susie will fall apart because her ballet lessons are the only thing that is giving her any stability and self-esteem at the moment.

If I'm the judge having to make decisions about your kids, I hate not knowing those things because I never have complete information; there just *never* is enough time.

If your case goes to trial, your trial will be, at best, nothing more than a single snapshot of your marriage. Think of your family photo album. How many of those snapshots reflect an accurate image of your family patterns? Would you really want your and your childrens' futures decided by those photos?

So, let's go back to the beginning. Is this the system you want to decide where your kids go to school, who gets kicked out of the house, and what bills get paid and by whom? Think about it.

12

What Happens When Your Spouse Hires the Lawyer from Hell?

You've just started your divorce. You've checked out the local bar association, interviewed several attorneys, and selected the one who seems to most closely match your goals of achieving a reasonable, quick and relatively healthy and inexpensive settlement of all your divorce issues. Your spouse then hires "the lawyer from hell."

What do you do?

I have already said that anyone can make one mistake. At the beginning of a divorce, you're scared, confused, being pulled hither and yon by conflicting advice from friends, relatives and, yes, even the lawyers you've consulted. You make the best choice you can under the circumstances and, part way into the divorce, find that you've made a choice you're no longer comfortable with. That I understand. But if it happens more than once, I question either your judgment or your motives.

When the party on the other side of my case retains a "lawyer from hell" (and we all know who they are), I know several things. I know the fees are going to be at least triple what they should have been. I know that what my client has told me about the other spouse ("he says he just wants to be fair") is probably not true and I know I had better buy myself some industrial-strength Alka Seltzer because I'm going to need it.

I believe people are drawn to the attorneys they want, whether consciously or unconsciously. When a new client comes in to see me and says, "I hear you're a real barracuda; I want to clean my husband out," I instantly know what I'm dealing with. That's a case I decline because I will never satisfy her. What she wants is part of her spouse's anatomy, and I'm not willing to be the surgeon. I will explain to the client that my business is to get what the law allows and my goal is to do it in such a way that it can be settled reasonably and quickly. I explain that although I am one hell of a good litigator, litigation is a last resort. If I don't get a response with which I am satisfied, I decline the case. I can only assume that when the same client goes to see the "lawyer from hell," she gets the reaction she wants. He may do some strutting and primping and bragging about track records and such, and that client is going to get precisely the lawyer she asked for.

Sometimes your spouse's lawyer takes a much more aggressive position than you expect. He may be telling you one thing ("I really want you to have the house") while his attorney is moving heaven and earth to get it sold out from under you. He may even tell you that he "can't do anything about it" because his attorney is telling him he *has to*. Nonsense. One of the things lawyers are paid to do is to take the heat for our clients. I understand that. I cannot tell you the number of times a client has said to me, "I really want to fight this because I think I'm right; but I don't want to tell my spouse how I feel, so I'm just going to say you're insisting I do it this way." If the thing the client wants me to do is consistent with my own goals and ethics, that's fine; if it isn't, I have an ex-client. But that process has also taught me that most people pick the lawyers they want and get the lawyers they deserve.

I have very little sympathy for a client who goes to an attorney, hires him under the premise that, "I hear you're a real shark and that's what I want" and then complains later that the "shark" turned on him. Excuse me . . . what did you think you were getting?

I have much more respect for the client who gets a second opinion because "I thought my attorney was going to promote settlement, but he just seems to be getting into a pissing contest with the other attorney."

There's an interesting note that goes with all of this. A prospective client will frequently consult with me and want to be sure that I really hate my opposing counsel. They somehow think that if I have personal animosity toward Attorney X, this will help their case. In fact, the reverse is true. The *last* thing you should be paying for is my personal vendetta. Why on earth should you pay me my hourly rate to score points on Attorney X because he offended me in the last case we had against each other? This is particularly true if it is in your best interests to settle. Enmity of a personal nature between the two attorneys only results in increased fees, ugly battles and delayed resolution.

Sometimes a litigant hires the attorney from hell out of fear. She knows he is a jerk, but is so afraid of her spouse that she thinks only a jerk can protect her. If you think your spouse might do this and want to forestall it, your best chance is to assure her that you really want to settle, that you want the divorce to be amicable and fair, and that you will do what it takes to see that it is. Then, *demonstrate* that you mean it by being utterly aboveboard at absolutely every opportunity.

So, when your spouse hires the "attorney from hell" and, more important, stays with him after a skirmish or two, my advice is this: take a closer look at your spouse. Whatever representations he or she may have made about wanting to be reasonable are not true. Each of us is responsible for the choices we make. If he has chosen someone who truly wants and intends to clean you out, and he doesn't either intervene or change attorneys, he is getting precisely the attorney he wants and the case is being run according to his plan.

A final note on the attorney from hell: if you have one on the other side of your case that is not the signal to go out and hire his clone to represent you. At the risk of sounding trite, two wrongs don't make a right. In this case, two wrongs will drive both of you to the poorhouse. Instead, keep playing the case straight and by the book on your side. It will be frustrating, of course, but when all is done, you will at least be able to like what you see in the mirror. The moral of this story is that just because your spouse has decided to be a jerk, you are not absolved from taking responsibility for your own choices and your own tactics.

13

Mediation and
No Fault

A trend is growing across the country in favor of mediation as a method of resolving family law disputes. This results from at least two factors. First, litigants are becoming much more sophisticated about alternative ways to resolve their disputes. Second, for reasons on which I am only too happy to expound at length, our court systems are quite unsuited to the practical and expedient resolution of most family law conflicts.

If you are considering divorce and your situation has not yet been polarized, you should at least consider mediation.

First, you need to know what mediation is and is not.

Mediation is not about both of you going to the same lawyer in a traditional sense. Instead, you jointly consult an individual who is trained in mediation, which is an entirely different process than adversarial law. Although many mediators are lawyers, they don't have to be.

Mediators cannot represent either side and may insist that each party independently consult with counsel, often during the course of the mediation and especially before an agreement is signed. The duty of the mediator is to assist the parties in reaching the agreement that works best for them, not to provide legal advice. In this way, the mediator takes the place of the court process but does not prevent the parties from obtaining information about their legal rights and crafting their own solutions.

I frequently get calls from prospective clients who want me to represent both sides. They obviously confuse dual representation with the mediation process. I consider it unethical to represent adversaries, though I know that there are attorneys who do not share my opinion. If I am functioning as an attorney, I have an obligation to my client, to be sure he is apprised of his legal rights. In dual representation, who is that? I would be faced with an ethical dilemma on every issue, because good advice to one party may be detrimental to the interests of the other.

In contrast, mediators don't represent either side. The best ones resolve this issue by insisting that each party have independent counsel. Therefore, the mediator can focus on the give and take that will promote a resolution of some or all of the outstanding issues.

In appropriate cases, mediation has numerous advantages over the traditional approach to litigation.

• It is private.

As I've indicated, courts are almost always open to the public. Although it is sometimes possible to seal court files or obtain a closed hearing, it is relatively rare. In mediation, however, all proceedings are closed and this can be a real benefit as it keeps your personal and financial business out of the public eye.

• It is cheaper.

You may ask how that can be when you are paying the fees of an additional professional. However, even if there are two consulting attorneys, their roles are radically redefined once you enter mediation. Discovery is usually informal and coordinated by the mediator rather than the infinitely more cumbersome and expensive traditional approach. The role of the consulting attorney is to advise participants of their legal rights and the consequences of the agreements being considered. This requires much less of their time. And since they are not required to pursue "due diligence" there is no incentive to over litigate the case to be certain they have looked under every rock. I have consulted with several mediators whom I respect, and they report that the average cost is about a third to a half of a fully litigated case. Thus, the parties keep more of the marital estate for themselves.

- It is quicker.

Formal discovery is not only expensive, it is slow. Time delays are built into the system, but they can be shortcut by the informal exchange of data required by the mediation process. Also, interim issues can be determined by your timetable, not the court's. Mediators have more time available than judges do. You won't have to wait weeks or months for an order for temporary support or interim custody, or take the risk that your case is continued because the judge ran out of time.

- It is creative.

This is probably the greatest single advantage of mediation. Most people don't realize that the judge's authority may be extremely limited. In a system based on legal precedent, the judge is likely to be bound to apply only one or two approaches to a particular problem. The truly elegant solution to the facts of your particular situation may well be deemed "abuse of discretion" by an appellate court if it doesn't fall within the parameters of the legal precedent which your trial judge is obliged to follow.

The truth is that on your worst day, you and your spouse can probably think of several better and more creative approaches to your problem than a judge is likely to impose. Mind you, it isn't because the judge is unwilling. Assuming the time is available, the judge would like nothing better than to find the perfect solution. The problem is that it may not be within the relatively narrow constraints of his discretion.

Before attempting mediation, there is one essential concept which is a precondition to success: You *must* recognize that mediation requires compromise. Both parties must be willing to do so or you are wasting your time and your money. If you are not willing to make concessions, even on things you think you should win, rethink your course and review Chapter 4, "Recipe for the Divorce from Hell." If you are honestly willing to compromise, proceed:

Choosing a Mediator

As in the choice of any other professional, it is important to do your homework in selecting a mediator. In any community, there are going to be some people who have proven track records as mediators. There is also a growing number of wannabes who have decided to become mediators because they can't make it in the world of adversarial law and think mediation is easier. If I am a litigant choosing a mediator, I can assure you that I want someone who is into mediation because he is very, very good at it and not because he failed at something else. The changing economics of the legal profession, coupled with increasing law school output and shrinking legal budgets, are causing more and more attorneys to find they simply can't make it in the world of adversarial law. They are often drawn to mediation as an alternative. Find out which category your prospective mediator falls into.

It is tough to do family law very well. A good family lawyer has to know not only the relevant statutes and case law, but also a great deal about other subjects, such as real estate transactions and tax. In addition, the lawyer must have a working knowledge of practical psychology. Add to that strong litigation skills and trial tactics and you have a rare bird, indeed. I have often said it is easy to practice mediocre family law and extremely difficult to do it well. Select someone who does mediation solely because he is very, very good at it and for no other reason. A good source for a referral to a mediator is probably your therapist.

The talents required of a good mediator are very different from those required by either a therapist or an adversarial lawyer. You may find an individual who happens to be good at both, but don't assume that it is so. A good mediator should be someone who is an effective listener and who can be creative enough to help both parties achieve most if not all of their goals. A good mediator is nonjudgmental and can achieve a balance of knowledge and power in the mediation process without favoring one side or the other.

There are two basic styles of mediation, one proactive and the other relentlessly neutral (you can tell where my personal bias lies). A proactive mediator will assist the parties to reach their own solution. However, if they get stuck, the mediator will suggest possible solutions, and will tell them what a court is likely to do in a similar situation. Other mediators feel it is inappropriate for them to make specific suggestions, and will refuse to do so. While I respect their reasons, I believe parties to mediation frequently need more guidance than they receive from a passive mediator. They don't know what a court is likely to do, and the mediator's experience can be an important resource in steering them to a creative solution.

After you have investigated mediators in your area, it is time to make an appointment for a consultation. Don't forget, however, that both parties must agree on the individual. Each mediator has a slightly different way of doing things. I would caution you, however, not to talk to the mediator individually until you have discussed it with your spouse. Doing so may make it impossible for you to sell this individual to the other party. Remember, we're all human. If you are already afraid that your spouse (whom you perceive is in a position of power) is going to pull a fast one on you, you will be very nervous if he's already had a conference with the proposed mediator. You will assume that he's already "gotten to" the mediator because it fits with your fear. Now, mind you, any professional, whether a mediator, custody evaluator, forensic accountant or anyone else who functions in divorce cases in a professional capacity will tell you it makes not one whit of difference who calls him first. Their job is to form their opinions objectively. But we are not talking about objective facts here; we're talking about fear. Therefore, if you want an agreement to a particular mediator, make the first appointment jointly. I also suggest that you and your spouse interview two or three of the top mediators before deciding. This ensures that both of you have had input in the selection and will increase the likelihood of a successful resolution.

Mediation works best when both parties are in relatively equal bargaining positions. By that I mean that you both have similar access to your family financial data, similar skill and ability in making business-type decisions and a relatively even balance of power. Small and sometimes large differences in power and knowledge can be balanced in the mediation process by a good mediator. Extreme differences such as an over-controlling bully or a person who is totally withdrawn usually cannot be. If one party has been a bully throughout the marriage, I don't think mediation is likely to succeed. The bully is unlikely to change his stripes during mediation and the mediator may be tempted to become an advocate for the weaker party, simply to restore equilibrium. I'm not saying don't try it, but I would look carefully at these factors. A good mediator can determine in two or three sessions whether mediation is likely to be successful.

Remember, too, that the role of a mediator is neither a referee nor an advocate. Therefore, don't get all excited if the mediator isn't "on your side." That isn't her job. She will be making every effort to be evenhanded and completely neutral in dealing with you and your spouse. Also, if you want your mediation to work, you will be well advised to focus on the issues to be resolved, and not get sidetracked into trying to prove what a jerk your spouse might have been. It may be true, but that is not the point.

It is a good idea for each side to have competent counsel throughout the mediation process. This is usually called a "consulting attorney." Virtually all mediators will advise you to have an attorney review the agreement before signing. Many will insist that you periodically consult with an attorney throughout the process. There is a very practical reason for this. You may be proceeding happily in the mediation process, making erroneous assumptions about the legal consequences of the agreement you are discussing. If you wait until a final agreement has been reached before consulting an attorney, and only then find out that your basic assumptions are wrong, I guarantee your spouse will feel double-crossed when you back out of what he thought was a "final" agreement.

By periodically consulting with independent counsel, you will educate yourself on the legal pitfalls of a proposal that is being discussed before committing to it. If you wait until the end and then refuse to sign the agreement because you've suddenly discovered it doesn't give you what you thought you were bargaining for, you will have wasted a great deal of time and money in mediation and created a huge reservoir of hard feelings. Do yourself a favor. Make sure you understand an agreement before you commit to it, even conditionally.

Finally, recognize that some cases simply are not suited to mediation. Mediation assumes first and foremost that both of you are being straight with one another, that you both are sharing information equally and no one is withholding any relevant financial or other data. It assumes that neither one of you is playing mind games to obtain an unfair advantage. And it assumes that you are each committed enough to the process to compromise and willing to let the other person win if it is not a cost to you.

No Fault

Most states now have some variation of no fault divorce. The definition will vary from jurisdiction to jurisdiction. In California, fault only creeps back into divorce tangentially in connection with some (but not most) custody disputes.

Check with your lawyer to find out what "no fault" means in your jurisdiction. In the meantime, here are some suggestions for some things that "no fault" probably *does not* mean.

- Since he walked out, I get the kids and the property.

- Since he wants the divorce and I don't, he has to pay for it.

- She left the home; it's abandonment.

- The courts aren't going to let her see the kids because she's committed adultery with her boyfriend and is, therefore, unfit.

Most states find "no fault" appealing because they recognize that it is in the interest of families to take "he said/she said" disputes out of the courts, where they probably never belonged anyway. Again, check with your lawyer. But whether your state is a community property or an equitable distribution state, most courts will try to remove the element of fault as much as possible from the distribution of property.

This means that if what you really want and need from the legal system is public vindication, you are likely to be disappointed. Instead of getting on the witness stand and telling the world chapter and verse about how you have been wronged, find another outlet for your venting. You are simply going to have to find another forum. I suggest you substitute your therapist's office or a lonely mountain top rather than mutual friends, a local billboard, your spouse's co-workers, his family or your children.

There is a distressing trend in some state legislatures to reintroduce fault into marital dissolution. Some legislators feel that the requirement of fault will deter divorce, and therefore "strengthen the institution of marriage" and aid children. I believe nothing could be farther from the truth. While these attempts are well intentioned, I am convinced that nothing will be more likely to firmly plant children in the middle of their parents' conflict that to tie a financial or other incentive to proof of "fault." Interestingly, these fault-based proposals are opposed by many mothers' groups and virtually all family lawyers. The Lawyer from Hell is, of course, an exception. He would love nothing better than to call out the private investigators and bill thousands of dollars to air somebody else's dirty laundry in public.

14

Special Masters, Court's Experts, Evaluators and Private Judges

There have been radical changes in recent years in the way in which cases are prepared and tried in court. As a result, there are a number of new terms with which you will need to be familiar.

In the old days, in a so-called "complicated" case, each party would retain their own team of expert witnesses who would then troop down to the courthouse and, as advocates, present "their" side of the case. This "battle of the experts" significantly increased the cost of trial and, all too frequently, left the court with very little more information than it had in the beginning with which to decide difficult issues.

The lunacy of this approach was particularly clear in custody cases. Mom would hire her expert who would meet only with her and with the kids who would testify that she was the greatest mother since the Virgin Mary. Dad would take the kids to his own expert when they were with him during visitation. His expert would then testify that Dad was Father of the Year. In all too many cases, the expert would only interview one party, so how *could* he have a balanced opinion? After all, if the standard for determination of custody is "best interests of the children," how can an expert witness who has only seen one party or who is in fact hired by and beholden to only one side be in the position of independence necessary to evaluate the best interests of the children?

As a result, more and more of the really good custody evaluators began to insist that they would work only as joint experts or as the court appointed expert. This preserves their independence and their ability to competently discharge their duty to represent the best interests of the children and not either party.

This is fast becoming the standard procedure for custody and visitation evaluators, and the approach has now spread to other areas of the law as well. Here are some definitions:

Custody Evaluator

This person is generally a psychologist, psychiatrist, social worker or a marriage, family and child counselor. Someone who serves in this capacity should be trained in developmental psychology, and have extensive experience in dealing with divorced families. Generally, they maintain a private practice in addition to court evaluation work. Sometimes they are known as "forensic" psychologists. Forensic simply means someone who is familiar with the law and presents information and recommendations in a way that is useful to the court.

The custody evaluator will be appointed to evaluate the family and make recommendations about the custodial or visitation arrangement which is in the best interests of the children. Generally they will prepare a written report summarizing their findings. Sometimes the report includes psychological testing of both parties (they should never test only one party) and/or they may test the children. Many will want to interview the children. This is covered in greater detail in Chapter 19 "Custody Evaluation."

The evaluator's task is to determine the attachments and relationships in the family, the characteristics of each member and the family dynamic. Good recommendations will not be based on an arbitrary formula; they will be custom-tailored to the family involved.

This is a very narrow subspecialty of psychotherapy. There are any number of people who are superb therapists who simply do not make good evaluators. The most important distinction between the two is that the evaluator has to be able to step back from the therapeutic desire to help the family heal and make the hard decision as to which custodial arrangement best serves the needs of the children. The assessment function is critical in a custody evaluation. Though remaining independent, a good evaluator will try to convey her recommendation, and the manner in which it was arrived at, as therapeutically as possible.

In virtually every case, at least one parent is not going to get what she wants from the recommendation. Frequently, *both* parents object. This means that, by definition, the evaluator is going to anger at least one and maybe both parents.

The evaluator has to withstand cross-examination and to think quickly. She must be clear about her conclusions and the factual basis for them, and be able to defend those conclusions to the satisfaction of the court. In other words, she has to be able to take the heat.

I have little respect for a so-called evaluator whose primary approach is to "cut the baby in half" so as to please both parents. This does nothing for the children and prolongs the conflict. I refer custody evaluations to highly qualified individuals, and I look to the evaluator to make the hard recommendation.

In most cases, two knowledgeable and experienced family lawyers will be able to agree on a competent joint expert. At least in my jurisdiction, we both know that we are wasting time and money in trying to line up "our own" experts since the court won't listen to them. We also all know who the good evaluators are. No, this doesn't mean that I prefer the evaluator who always comes down on the side of my client. In fact, the evaluator to whom I probably refer more often than any other is selected for precisely the opposite reason. I know that I can trust him to do what is, in his opinion, best for the kids regardless of what pressure Mom or Dad or Mom's or Dad's attorney applies. I respect that enormously. So, before referring a couple to him, I look twice at my own client, swallow hard in case I have misread the situation and I have the bad guy, and pick up the phone.

In any given location, there will probably be a pool of as few as two or three and as many as 15 or 20 therapists with whom all of the family lawyers have had experience and whose credentials and expertise are well known. These will be people who are very comfortable in a courtroom and will have demonstrated an ability to make the hard decision and stand behind it. They will not be "hired guns" who will support whichever parent or attorney applies the strongest pressure or who pays the bill. We all know who those people are, too, and they frankly don't get much respect either from the attorneys or from the courts.

After an evaluation, most cases settle without having to go to trial. The reason is obvious. I always caution my client that if the report of the independent evaluator comes down against him, he will have a huge uphill battle at trial. This is not to say that the evaluator is always right or that reports can't be challenged. However, one of the reasons it is so important to start out with a very good evaluator is that the court is going find an independent evaluation much more persuasive than one which is commissioned after the fact by the party who "lost" with the independent.

I am reminded of a local family law judge who stopped me in the hall one afternoon after I had just finished trying a particularly nasty custody case, and commented "Sue, you always bring me the hard ones." Of course I do . . . if it weren't hard, I wouldn't need a trial after the evaluation; I would have settled it.

There is another important benefit to having a joint custody evaluator. Kids have no business in a court of law, even in chambers. There is an old family law cartoon where Mother has taken the little boy into the courtroom. She stands in front of the bench, leans over and admonishes him "Now, honey, tell the nice judge what a son-of-a-bitch Daddy is." Very few judges will allow children in court and few evaluators are going to ask young children to choose which parent they want to live with (and the fact is that older children are likely to "vote with their feet"). The good news is that the evaluator has more specialized training and has much more time than the judge to meet with you, your spouse, and the children, and therefore gather as much information as he or she feels is essential to make a good recommendation. Assuming you have a competent evaluator, you are going to get a much better recommendation and a more thorough review of the facts than if you simply take it into court and let each party explain why they should have custody of the kids.

My comments have been primarily directed toward private evaluators. Most counties in fact have publicly funded evaluation departments, sometimes called Family Court Services or Conciliation Courts. The caution is that there are wide variations in the funding and the administration of these offices, which directly impact the quality of the resulting evaluation. Some counties have substantial budgets which not only allow them to hire highly qualified people who are enthusiastic about their jobs, but also allocate the time necessary to do a thorough evaluation.

Other counties are so under funded that they simply can't offer competitive salaries to lure the truly good people and don't have the staff time available to do a complete evaluation. If you are facing a custody dispute, you should be sure and ask your attorney about the practice in your county so you can make an informed decision.

Forensic Accountant

A forensic accountant is usually a certified public accountant who testifies in court on financial, tax and accounting issues. In a divorce, these topics typically include the valuation of a business which is subject to division at trial, the availability of income for support or tracing of separate and joint contributions into various assets. Sometimes the tax consequences of the disposition of an asset will be a primary issue at trial. If any of these are potential problems in your case, your attorney will probably suggest consulting a forensic CPA. Again, this is a relatively limited pool of people who are not only highly experienced in divorce taxation (and, believe me, this is a real substantive specialty) but people who are also comfortable testifying at court. Frankly, to be cross-examined in public by someone whose job it is to make you look like an idiot is not a particularly pleasant experience for most people. Therefore, it is important to find an accountant who not only knows divorce taxation (and more specifically the area of divorce finance relevant to *your* case) but who also has substantial court-room experience.

I teach seminars for forensic CPAs, and am finding that lots of accountants are now trying to break into forensic work for a number of reasons, sometimes purely economic. It takes years to learn the nuances of divorce accounting. The person who does your tax return is probably not a good choice unless you happen to have your returns done by someone who also has a thriving forensic divorce accounting subspecialty.

As with custody evaluators, there will probably be a relatively small pool of highly respected forensic accountants in your area. There will be a much larger pool of part-time or "wannabe" experts and, with luck, some rising stars who will work at lower rates.

If your divorce is likely to include issues of business valuation and division, the valuation of stock options, partnership buyouts and the like, your attorney should be talking to you about consulting an accountant. Find out who the top local experts are. You will want to know what they do, what experience they have and why your attorney thinks one would be more appropriate than another for your case.

If you or your attorney suspects the tax returns are fraudulent, you may need someone who can review them and advise you. If your or your mate's income situation is highly complicated, for example if large amounts of income are routinely derived from capital gains or unusual business transactions, you may well need a forensic accountant to sort all of that out so that the court can make an appropriate support order. More and more frequently now, accountants are retained to determine the marital standard of living for purposes of ongoing spousal support or alimony. Finally, the property division may create, in and of itself, tax consequences to you or your spouse. As with any complex financial litigation, you should be advised by a forensic CPA, whether or not you intend to use this person at trial. It is simply part of evaluating a complicated financial situation and making sure that you are making good decisions regarding settlement and/or trial.

Suppose you find you simply can't afford one of the top forensic CPAs, but you really need expert assistance in your case. You do have a couple of options.

First, you may be able to get by with a limited evaluation from the expert. This means that rather than doing a full blown "by the book" business evaluation, you limit the areas they look into or ask for a "ballpark" or range of values based on certain assumptions. Of course, you have to be sure you are comfortable with the assumptions used. This generally results in the expenditure of significantly less time by the expert, and a resulting lower total fee. You may also ask if there is an associate in the expert's office who can do the work under supervision at a lower hourly rate.

Alternatively, ask your lawyer who the rising stars are in the next generation of experts. You may be able to find someone who is newer to the profession, charges a lower hourly rate, and makes up for it in enthusiasm. Someone who is young and building a reputation will want to do an excellent job to create future referrals. Don't confuse this person with the "wannabe," however. The person I'm referring to here is not merely dabbling. He's striving mightily to enter the ranks of the top forensics, and wants to do it as quickly as possible.

Discuss all of these possibilities with your attorney, along with the possibility of using a joint expert to control the cost.

The idea of joint experts is a little later in coming to the financial arena than it was in custody. I have seen a definite trend in the last ten years in favor of either "joint" or "court's" experts. Some judges will blatantly tell litigants not to bother retaining their own separate forensic CPAs because the court is going to appoint its own expert. If your county is one of those, don't waste your money on "your own" expert. If the court's expert disagrees with yours, guess whose opinion is going to carry the greatest weight with the judge? Again, most experienced family law attorneys will seriously consider a joint or court's expert. If the other side refuses to agree, in most jurisdictions you can file a motion with the court asking the court to appoint an independent expert rather than have the duplicate work and expense of two separate evaluations.

A word of caution: Once you are armed with this information from your initial contact with your prospective new attorney, *don't* call the expert yourself to "sound her out." Doing so will taint her for a joint appointment. This means that if you decide that you would like to have this person do the work, chances are she won't be independent anymore because you talked to her before she was jointly retained. Even if you didn't get any particularly useful information from her or she from you, your spouse may be so paranoid that you might have "gotten to" the candidate that they refuse to agree to her appointment. Therefore, don't ever call a prospective forensic evaluator or expert, whether for custody, visitation, financial or any other matters, until your attorney has instructed you to do so. The legal culture varies widely from jurisdiction to jurisdiction and the last thing you want to do is find out that you have just discovered the absolutely perfect person who understands your case and will do the evaluation for a fraction of what everyone else is charging, only to find that he can't accept the appointment because you have already talked to him and he is therefore no longer "independent."

Special Masters and Referees

These are terms which are used somewhat interchangeably in various jurisdictions. If your attorney uses one of them, ask him to define it for you.

Generally, a special master or a referee is someone who is deputized by the court to make certain findings, or at the least make a recommendation to the court on a complicated issue. This is different from an expert witness who will evaluate the situation and then testify as to his conclusions. He is giving an opinion, but he doesn't have decision making power. In contrast, the court's power may be delegated in large degree to a special master or referee. The special master makes a specific recommendation, which carries great weight with the court.

There are a number of situations where a special master or referee (and I am going to use the term special master to refer to both) is a very good thing to have.

For example, suppose you have a highly complex family-owned business which constitutes the primary marital asset. The value of the business and the decision as to who should get it in the divorce depends entirely on the trier of fact (that is, the person making the decision) being sophisticated in the areas of goodwill evaluation, tax or stock options. Now it is just possible that your family law judge, before being appointed to the bench, had a flourishing practice involving stock options, and therefore understands the legal nuances. However, it is much more likely that he was a District Attorney prosecuting drug dealers and doesn't know a Schedule C from vitamin C. Now, I'm not saying that former District Attorneys do not make good family law judges; in fact, some of the best family law judges I have seen started out as criminal lawyers. One doesn't learn overnight to read a tax return or spot a phony balance sheet. With the best intent in the world, the brightest judge will not see all of the implications of the evidence being presented if the subject matter is new to him. Therefore, in many cases, I will in fact invite the court to appoint someone who is an expert in these areas to make the decision instead of the judge.

In some jurisdictions, the special master can only report her findings to the court who then must make the final decision. However, as a practical matter the special master often has all but judicial powers. This can be wonderful, and in most cases I think it is. It can be dreadful if the person to whom the power is delegated is biased or is not as sophisticated as he pretends to be. Therefore, it is important for you (or more particularly for your attorney) to know who is likely to be appointed special master and whether that individual's background and training qualify him to evaluate the evidence and make and appropriate decision.

In my county, there is a small pool of accountants whom the courts routinely appoint for this type of work. I am advised that in other areas, the practice is growing but not nearly as advanced as it is in the Bay Area. Whatever your jurisdiction, if this sounds like your case, ask your attorney about the practice in your local court.

Evaluators, forensic experts and special masters are all valuable resources in proper cases. They can also be misused when judicial power is improperly delegated. All in all, however, they significantly streamline judicial proceedings. They have the advantages of specialized training and expertise as well as significantly more time than the judge. As a result, they can resolve a complicated problem more efficiently. You will pay for their expertise, however. Frankly, I would rather have a competent expert take as much time as necessary to make the right decision, rather than the most brilliant judge in the world try to decide too quickly on too little evidence because there simply isn't the time to present it properly.

There is an emerging field for special masters in high-conflict custody and visitation cases. Some parents choose to fight about every facet of their children's lives long after the divorce is over. In some cases, the court will appoint an individual (usually an experienced custody evaluator) to be either a special master or a mediator of post-dissolution disputes involving the children. This is to ensure that every conflict doesn't result in the filing of a new motion and a series of court hearings. Instead, the order will provide that neither party may raise a non-emergency issue involving the children until they have first attempted to resolve it through the appointed mediator or special master. Sometimes the special master has the power to make the decision, sometimes just to report and make recommendations to the court. In either event, it is a powerful tool for keeping litigious families out of court over relatively minor issues. Of course, the parties are ordered to pay the fees of the special master, which also has a chilling effect on making a federal case over how Johnny's hair is cut.

Private Judges

One of the recent developments in response to crowded court calendars is the increasing use of private judges (also called "rent-a-judges" or judges "pro tem"). Judge "pro tem" simply means someone is appointed a judge "for a time." In such a case, the trial or some part of it is assigned to a judge who is hired by the parties. A private judge may be a retired judge who works part time on a case by case basis. A "judge pro-tem" is usually an attorney who is hired on an hourly basis to hear a particular case, usually in his own office.

Except for those jurisdictions (such as mine) where there is a successful program of attorneys who volunteer their time to sit pro tem, these individuals will expect to be paid. In many cases, the payment will be well worth the cost.

Your attorney may recommend hiring a private judge for your case. There are many good reasons for doing so. Perhaps he does not believe that the judge to whom your case is assigned has sufficient expertise in a particular area of the law. It may be that in your jurisdiction, it will take many months or even years to obtain a trial date long enough to accommodate your case and the delay does not justify the financial and emotional hardship. Also, a case heard by a private judge is just that, private, and not open to the public.

In any event, careful research is required before selecting an individual.

The first thing you need to know is that both attorneys will have to agree on the private judge. For obvious reasons of bias, it is simply impossible for one side to unilaterally hire the judge.

Second, there is a wide variation in the capabilities of the judges who may be selected.

Most private judges have served for many years on the bench and are simply supplementing their retirement income by doing private judging on a part time basis after retiring. They may be highly qualified in divorce law. On the other hand, they may be total novices when it comes to your particular issue, having spent 20 years handling criminal cases. Find out the difference before hiring one for your case.

One of the beauties of private judging is that you have a choice. If you are simply assigned to a judge at the courthouse, you generally have little to say about it. Not so with private judges. There are, of course, some pitfalls with retired judges. If I tried a case before them when they were on the Superior Court bench and was not impressed, I can assure you they won't get my nod. Also, it is important to be comfortable that they have kept up with changes in the law since retiring. I would want to know that the private judge I am agreeing to is not only experienced in family law matters but has recent family law experience. The law can change very quickly. I would also want to know about any known biases or idiosyncracies. If the suggested judge is unfamiliar to me or from a different county, I would do some research before agreeing that this is the person who will hear my client's case.

With a private attorney or "judge pro tem," the procedure is a little different. My county has an extremely active judge pro tem program where experienced family lawyers agree to volunteer a few days per year to hear family law cases. We do this so that the courts stay open when the local judges are on vacation or taking (or teaching) classes, or simply to alleviate the press of overcrowded court calendars. We recognize that families frequently can't afford to wait for immediate restraining or support orders, and by agreeing to serve occasionally as a judge pro tem, we can help ease the delay in the calendar and to promote early resolution of cases. I donate my time frequently as do many others. If your county has a program such as this, you may want to look into the availability of a volunteer judge pro tem. As with any private judge, both sides would have to agree to the specific individual and that agreement would have to be in writing and signed by both attorneys.

You should still do the research regarding the specific expertise of the proposed judge. On a highly technical issue, however, I almost always prefer a highly experienced family lawyer to a judge (however brilliant) with limited family law experience.

If you elect to proceed through private judging, there are some decisions which you will have to make. One of these is the formality of the proceedings. Specifically, you will need to determine whether to preserve your right to appeal the decision if you disagree with it.

If your case is heard before a regularly scheduled judge pro tem in the courthouse, there may well be a court reporter available. This means that either party will have a record on appeal if they wish to dispute the judge's opinion.

If, on the other hand, you retain a private judge, either of the retired version or a judge pro tem who operates out of his own office, you must decide whether to have a court reporter present. Doing so will increase the expense. On the other hand, if you do not have a written record and the private judge makes a mistake, it is almost impossible to successfully pursue an appeal. Again, this is a cost/benefit analysis which you should discuss with your attorney.

There is one other use for private judges or special masters which is just becoming popular. Some of these individuals have developed such expertise and credibility that they are retained as private settlement judges. Frequently, we don't want to tip our hand on a sensitive issue by having a settlement conference before the judge who will try the case. If both sides have confidence in the individual, it is frequently useful to have an informal settlement conference before the expert. This is a wonderful way to test the strength of your case without going to court and getting destroyed. Again, it takes a special individual and both sides have to agree, but I have settled some very difficult and complex cases this way, and the clients didn't have to pay for expensive trial preparation time.

Part III

What About
the Kids?

15

Kids Aren't
Jelly Jars

One of the most painful realities faced by any parent contemplating divorce is the certainty that for large blocks of time in the future, your kids will not be with you. This is true whether or not you are likely to become the custodial parent. The children have been with you since birth, and the fear that they won't be in the future can be paralyzing. *Don't* let that fear cause you to turn your children's bodies and souls into a battleground.

Countless parents have said to me, "I want 50/50 custody; that's *my* right." Nonsense. It's theirs.

Kids are not fungible possessions which can be divided equally, such as pots and pans, bank accounts and place settings of sterling flatware. Kids are people, small and highly vulnerable people. A divorce turns their world upside down and they are terrified that they won't see Mom *or* Dad again. They are utterly powerless and don't understand why this awful thing is happening. How you, as parents, handle your responsibility to them will greatly influence whether your children come through the process healthy, well-adjusted and feeling loved or so scarred that they turn into miserable parents themselves and repeat the same patterns with their own children.

There is a huge difference between "I'm entitled to 50% time with my children," and the real truth, which is that the *children* are *entitled* to two parents. This simple fact escapes all too many parents and their children pay the price. It's the kids' right, not Mom's or Dad's.

I would like to say that the divorce process can make good parents out of bad ones, but that is only occasionally true. Sometimes divorce is a wake-up call to parents who have been largely absent from their childrens' day-to-day lives. They suddenly realize what they and their children have been missing and educate themselves about how best to assume an active and positive parenting role. I always encourage them, no matter how belated their change of heart; the children can only benefit. The good news is that even if you haven't been Parent of the Year in the past, you have a second chance. You have an opportunity through the process of divorce to create a new relationship with your children, to love, nurture and support them, not because it is your right, but because it is theirs.

So what happens when someone actually does decide, in the throes of a divorce, to start being a better parent? The other parent all too often treats this reversal as a personal betrayal. It is amazing how often the parent who has been the primary caretaker is angry and resentful, bitterly complaining that her former partner is turning into a good parent, as though that is a bad thing. She'll protest endlessly that the very person who refused to attend soccer practices and ballet recitals now insists on coaching the team and schlepping tu-tus to dance lessons, treating the turnaround as a dirty trick. Of course, these are the same people who want gold stars for marital suffering. I submit that the parent who has been carrying the burden of these activities should be grateful that the other has decided to become responsible, however tardily.

In these days of increasing joint custody, all too many parents become obsessed with marking calendars and counting days and hours (even sleep hours!) in order to calculate their actual percentage of time with the children. Sometimes they are motivated by a desire to increase or reduce the child support, sometimes just to keep score. Many state legislatures have quite deliberately tinkered with child support guidelines to reduce or eliminate the financial incentive to fight for additional timeshare. They have done this by reducing the incremental reduction in child support as the noncustodial parent's percentage of timeshare increases. Some states give no financial credit at all for timeshare. In others, the support will still be reduced somewhat, but not pro rata. The net result is that a noncustodial parent who wants more time with the children may suffer a real financial hardship. The legislatures which have adopted this philosophy do it intentionally. They don't want parents fighting for custody to save money on support, and if that means that noncustodial parents bear a greater proportion of the financial burden, so be it. The unfortunate cost is that the almost-but-not-quite equal custodial parent doesn't get the break he probably should financially. On the other hand, only a lunatic would fight for custody to save a few bucks on support, although a distressing number of parents do precisely that.

When a prospective client calls and says he has "27%," or 33%, or 36%, I cringe. Someone has an agenda, and it has nothing to do with the kids. Not once have I heard a kid worry about whether they spend 24% or 28% of their time with Dad or with Mom, but I've had to litigate it when it made a difference in the child support. True, the percentage is important to some parents because they want tangible, quantifiable evidence that they are still actively involved in their child's lives. It's never the child's agenda, though. Kids couldn't care less about percentages; what they are interested in is the love, concern and attention they receive from both parents.

Many custody conflicts are traceable to a fear that if you don't have custody, you won't see your kids. I have found that some of these can be avoided at the outset simply by making certain that the noncustodial parent (for want of a better term) knows that he will still have frequent and continuing contact with the children. He is less likely, therefore, to pursue custody for defensive reasons. Many parents know in their heart of hearts that the children (at least at this stage of their development) are probably better off in the other household. Nevertheless, they pursue custody out of fear. In these cases, the litigation can frequently be averted if they are assured that they are not giving up their rights forever and that they will still get frequent contact with the children. If they can be sufficiently reassured, the children may not be made pawns.

It is also important to note that custody is never permanent. The courts and the custody evaluators who make the recommendations now realize that childrens' needs change as they develop. Each child is unique, and individuals within a single family may have vastly different requirements. Recognize that custody is a fluid and elastic concept. The sooner you and your spouse can accept this fact for the sake of the kids, the better it will be for all of you.

Remember that you and your spouse will be parents of these children forever. Don't make the children choose between you. If you don't know how to tell your children you're getting a divorce, see a therapist and get some suggestions from an expert. Let your children know in every possible way that you love them, that you care for them, that you are not divorcing them and, most important, that the divorce *is not their fault*. There are now many helpful books, pamphlets and videos available for explaining divorce to kids and dealing with their inevitable fears and questions. Research these, find them and implement the suggestions you find there. Some good ones are listed in Chapter 44, "More Resources."

Make a deal with your spouse that "kid issues" and "kid" conversations will never, repeat *NEVER* be dragged into money and support issues. I cannot state this strongly enough.

One of the most useful techniques I have found is for the parents to agree on a code. If either party starts a conversation with "This is a kid issue," or "This is a kid conversation," it's absolutely *verboten* to mention money. I don't care if the support check is two months late and the electricity is about to be turned off; I don't care if there's an offer on the house and you need to decide right now whether to accept it and how the proceeds are going to be divvied up; I don't care how irresistible the temptation to rehash for the fiftieth time the "how dare you leave me and what are you doing with that slut" conversation — resist the impulse. This rule has no exceptions. When the code is used, it means that "kid" issues are discussed first and, to the extent that you can, they are discussed dispassionately and calmly. If there are other pressing matters to be discussed, I suggest that you hang up the phone and dial one another again. It may sound silly, but this technique is successful because it is a very tangible, physical reminder that bleed-through between kid issues and money issues is not acceptable.

Despite the obvious benefits to the kids of having two parents jointly involved in the ongoing and inevitable problems of child-rearing, there are very practical benefits to the parents as well. Neither parent will be dissuaded from discussing a legitimate parenting issue for fear that the marital history will be rehashed. It is more important that each of you be free to call the other to report that Johnny is getting a "D" in math and we have to do something about it, without fear of repercussions. Otherwise, the call is not made, and the conflict escalates, all to the detriment of the child.

It works like this: assume Johnny's math grade comes in, and Mom knows that Dad should be told so they can address the issue constructively and consistently. However, every time she calls Dad, she has to listen to his anger at her for leaving him. Not surprisingly, she doesn't want to hear it again, so she doesn't call. Dad finds out after Johnny flunks math. He then feels that Mom is abusing her custodial power by shutting him out of Johnny's life and keeping legitimate information from him. He concludes that the only way to be sure he has ongoing input in Johnny's education is to insist on custody. Or perhaps he doesn't start a custody proceeding, but begins hounding the school for direct information, which makes the teacher, principal and, yes, Johnny, feel they are caught in the middle of a dispute that is not of their making. You get my drift.

And while all this is going on, don't forget that your kids are experiencing totally ordinary developmental problems which may account for their behavior changes. Developmental stages are just that, and not the other parent's fault. If you and your spouse were still together, Johnny might just as well be acting out at this phase, so don't automatically run to the courthouse asking for a reduction in contact with the other parent because your child is behaving differently than he did a year ago. He's growing, even in the middle of your divorce. Guess what. . . ? A 15-year-old is going to be 15 (oh, joy) whether or not Mom and Dad are divorcing. Recognize that, and don't assume the problem is the other parent's fault.

Suppose your spouse is pursuing custody solely to get a break on support or to pressure you to concede property issues in exchange for the custodial arrangement that you both know is in your children's best interests. I would like to say that I have a magic answer for this one. The process of divorce does not of itself turn bad parents into good ones, though some marginal parents wake up and learn from their mistakes. However, we rarely see a complete personality change. Someone who was an uncaring and inattentive parent prior to the separation is not likely to become a model one simply because the two of you are no longer together.

You may, in fact, have the opposite problem. Rather than trying to take the kids away from you, he may simply be absent. The courts cannot legislate good parenting. Be real. It's not the divorce that caused the problem. If your mate was a lousy parent when you were together, he is unlikely to turn into Father Knows Best afterward. You can't force him to visit. In that case, my guess is that you would have been raising the kids by yourself even if you had stayed married.

I can only offer you this observation: this is the person with whom you chose to have children. Obviously when you made that choice (or at some time since) you had to face the reality that you were going to have to do it alone. That's the truth. The consolation is that there are many highly responsible adults who only had one good parental role model. If it's the right one, one is all it takes.

Terrible Reasons to Fight for Custody

- I'll save money on child support because I can raise them for less than the support guideline calls for.

- I won't have my children around "that woman."

- I have more money and can provide the fancier home.

- I don't approve of her morals.

- Social pressure: "What's wrong with *her*? I heard she doesn't have custody of her children!"

Many custody fights are traceable to all the wrong reasons. The parents may be motivated by a continuation of the marital issues, usually power and control or hurt feelings, vengeance, unrequited love and the like. They may feel they can achieve financial gain, i.e., an adjustment in support in relation to timeshare. Sometimes it is fear of social censure: what will the neighbors think if I don't have custody?

Your spouse may have done any number of terrible things. He may be sleeping with someone else; his house may be a mess; he may cheat on his taxes. All this may have little or nothing to do with parenting skills. As strange as it may seem, an individual can, in fact be mentally ill, and still be the better (indeed, sometimes exemplary) parent. Your mate's conduct may mightily offend your sensibilities, but if it does not adversely affect the children, so what? The issue is the impact on the kids. On the other hand, if your spouse is flaunting her boyfriend in front of the children and the *children* (as opposed to you) are having a hard time accepting it, that's legit. If you're simply suffering from sexual jealousy yourself, go see a therapist and deal with it there. Don't make the kids the focus.

Suppose your spouse's house reminds you of a fraternity dorm. Well, I'm sure it's going to come as a great surprise that many perfectly well adjusted people were raised in log cabins with dirt floors. A little clutter was never at the top of any kid's list of complaints. If you know that your spouse can provide a warm, loving and nurturing environment for your kids, whether or not it would win a Good Housekeeping seal is irrelevant.

The issue of social pressure and sexual stereotyping is insidious. This was brought home to me years ago when I returned to my office after having won a particularly difficult custody case for my client (the father). A longtime employee (female) immediately asked, "what is wrong with the mother?" I was insulted at the implication that the only reason a father would win custody was that the mother was somehow defective. After I recovered from the denigration of my legal skills, it occurred to me that this comment came from someone who had been around the legal business for years and (I felt) should have known better. It taught me that social stereotypes are very deeply ingrained.

I hope we are getting to a point where a mother who knows in her heart that the kids are better off with Dad will feel freer to let that happen rather than subject the kids to a battle for fear of what the neighbors will say. Think about this: the better parent may well be the one who can be honest enough admit that the kids really need the other parent more and let them go rather than subject them to a bitter custody fight. That parent is really putting the kids' needs first.

Instead of plotting a power play for the kids or obsessing about what's wrong with your spouse, why not focus on your children? Redirect the energy spent vilifying your ex into planning an outing with your kids. The last I heard, it didn't cost a lot of money to be a good parent. It does, however, require effort. Go for a bike ride, build a model plane, or just *listen*. You'd be amazed how many people who have lived in the same house with their kids for years have never learned how to listen to them. Attend a parenting workshop. Get creative. And above all, get real. An 8-year-old may like nothing better than to go for a hike with you or just have your undivided attention. A 16-year-old is probably not going to want to chew the fat with a parent when he can be out with his friends, but you can still be available to him.

16

Joint
Custody

Most states have some variation of joint custody. I find there is a great deal of confusion about what it does and does not mean.

In the first place, it does not mean that every parent has a "right" to 50% timeshare. It represents a recognition that it is generally in the children's best interests to have frequent and continuing contact with both parents. That may mean 30% timeshare or 50% or some other number. Don't get sidetracked on counting days and hours to figure out the exact percentage, and above all, don't start counting sleep and school hours to prove your point.

People frequently assume that if there's joint custody, there will be no child support; not necessarily so.

If you want joint custody, you'll need to carefully discuss the implications with your attorney. Consider the following:

• You may well end up paying close to the same child support, notwithstanding the fact that you have to provide a home for the children as well.

• Can you really make room in your schedule for the kids' demands?

Children require time and attention. If you're not used to being the primary care giver, your life is going to change radically. Lose 10 points if your response is "I'll just hire a nanny and a cook."

- Recognize that you will have to deal with your spouse over the kids.

This is the case even if one of you is the primary custodian. If you have joint custody, you'll be communicating with each other all the time. Can you put your own differences aside in order to do this for the sake of the kids?

Joint custody doesn't necessarily mean the children spend equal time with each parent. It doesn't necessarily mean one week on, one week off. In fact, that is rarely the case. Most of the alternating week arrangements I have seen were negotiated by the parents, who were more concerned about being "fair"with each other than with determining the schedule which worked best for the children. Little kids don't always react well to constant shifts in where they sleep. Some are more adaptable than others, but you'll have to tailor the arrangement to the kids' needs, not some arbitrary sense of "fairness" between you and the other parent. Remember, kids aren't property; they are people.

I have seen true 50/50 custody work, but it requires two committed parents. More likely, it turns out to be 60/40 or something akin to that. If parents are too concerned about the percentage of time the kids are with them, especially as they get closer to an even split, they are probably more interested in keeping score with each other than in the children's needs.

Someone may suggest an arrangement to you which is called "birds' nesting." This means that the kids stay put and the parents move in and out of the house at regular intervals. I have never seen a court order this, but have occasionally had parents work it out on their own. It is extremely difficult to do successfully. It seems to work best for a *short* period at the beginning of the separation, while you're trying to work out the financial separation or while the house is being sold. It requires two parents who are absolutely committed to respecting each other's privacy. If either of you is not, this arrangement is doomed from the start.

You may be considering split custody. This means that each of the kids has a different visitation schedule. Children have different needs, and sometimes that means that one visits more (or longer) than his sibling. This arrangement can even be advantageous from time to time, as each child gets one on one time with each parent. It needs to be carefully tailored to your kids' needs, however.

If you're considering joint custody (and except for situations involving abuse, I recommend you try it), consider the scheduling carefully. Make sure that you and your spouse are putting the kids' needs first. At the risk of sounding trite, it's the quality of the time that matters more than the quantity.

17

Visitation Games, or How to Ensure Your Kids Will Resent You Forever

There are people who, once they have divided the property and fixed the support, can't resist continuing to fight with one another. These are the couples who seem to feel that *any* relationship with each other, even a hostile one, is better than none. If they have children, there is going to be a ready-made battleground. Even after custody is decided and a visitation order is in place, there are a million ways in which they can push one another's buttons to continue the war. When they do, the kids pay a horrendous price.

The best visitation order is a flexible one. When I see an order that says "Reasonable visitation on suitable advance notice" which *works*, I know I am dealing with two relatively responsible and adult parents. On the other hand, the more detailed the visitation order has to be, the more likely it is that the parents have a separate agenda. I once saw an order that ran to eight pages (single spaced) and delineated the precise time and location of drop off and pick up of every single visit, including how many hours the visiting parent had with the kids on Halloween (and whether those hours were before or after dark and with or without costume). I immediately knew that at least one (and possibly both) of the parents couldn't care less about the kids. It was a written power struggle, not a visitation schedule. To parents like this, the kids are not people at all. They are nothing but a new form of turf war.

I'm going to give you a whole list of things not to do to your kids around visitation. Before I do, there are a few things which you need to understand.

First, recognize that your kids are generally going to want to see the other parent. This is not a betrayal of you. Even if they are furious adolescents who are taking out their rage at the family breakup on the noncustodial parent, at some level they probably want contact. They are just too angry to see it or act on it. If you are the caretaker parent and the other has been absent, don't get your feelings hurt if the kids suddenly express a desire to spend more time with your ex. It's healthy and is not a reflection on the care and the love that you have given them. Don't turn it into a loyalty issue. It does not mean that they love you less, but rather that they have needs which, as good as you are as a parent, you cannot meet. This is the reality. You cannot completely fill the roles of both father and mother to your children, try as you might.

If you are the custodial parent, don't get too excited about the fact that the kids are a little nervous and upset, or tired or crabby when they come back from visitation. Don't go running into your attorney's office on Monday morning complaining that the kids should visit less because they returned tired and whiny. They will. The upset is usually caused by the fact that each transition between households underscores again the reality that Mom and Dad don't live in the same place anymore. They may become depressed at each transition. The cause of the depression, however, is that a transition is necessary at all. Don't use this normal reaction on the part of your child to try to restrict the visiting parent's time. Recognize it as a normal process and deal with it as best you can.

As hard as it is, keep your kid's needs first. The kids can't be with both of you every Christmas. You are going to have some lonely Christmases when you would give anything to be watching them open their presents. You won't be there. On an equal number of Christmases, your spouse will be experiencing the same loss. Do the sensible thing and have two Christmases (or birthdays or Hannukkas or whatever). Make sure that whatever the visitation arrangement, to the extent that it is possible, the kids are with Dad on Father's Day and with Mom on Mother's Day. This only makes sense.

Above all, let them know that it's OK to want to be with the other parent and you don't view it as a betrayal. You don't have to say a word to them to communicate how you really feel; kids pick up their parents' feelings through the airwaves. So don't get all sanctimonious about "I've never said a *word* about how I feel to the kids," when you have been conveying it every way you know through looks, sighs, sarcastic asides or conversations with your friends in their hearing. Please do your kids a favor and let it be safe for them to let you know they love both of their parents and not just you.

Failing all of the above, if you really want to make sure that your kids are going to resent you forever, here are some suggestions:

• Promise your kids some rare treat and then blame the other parent for the fact that it didn't come off.

"I was going to take you to Marine World last weekend, but your Mom wouldn't let you go." Or do the reverse, when you know the kids are already committed to go to the other parent's house, let them know that you had this wonderful opportunity to take them someplace special but couldn't because, "The judge says you have to go see your Dad."

• Schedule soccer, summer camp, or some other rigidly scheduled activity for the only time in the summer when the kids can visit the other parent at a distant location.

• Send only ill-fitting, torn and crummy clothes to the visiting parent's home.

Or, if you are the visiting parent, refuse to return the good clothes and send only the crummy ones back. Or, buy good clothes for the kids but insist they leave them at your house.

- Don't let the kids take their favorite toys on the visits or, if you are the visiting parent, buy all sorts of great toys for them, but insist that they can only play with them at your house.

This may mean that the kids want to show up for visitation more often in the short term because of all the neat stuff at your house, but don't flatter yourself: it has nothing to do with *you*.

- Make them leave their special things at your house.

This sends a clear message that their "stuff" isn't safe with the other parent.

- Create a scene at each transfer.

Use the opportunity of the kids being picked up or dropped off to berate the other parent about unrelated issues. This will guarantee that the kids have a real knot in their stomachs long before the transfer takes place.

- Dispose of your kid's pet while he is visiting the other parent (yes, I have actually seen someone do this).

He is going to be scared to death to ever go on another visit for fear that his new pet will go down, too. Imagine how the kid is going to feel when he comes running into the house looking for Fido only to find out that Fido bit the dust three days ago because you couldn't stand having him around. That's one that will have your kid in therapy till the age of 45.

- Insist that every holiday, every birthday party, even the school pageant becomes an opportunity for a confrontation.

Suppose Jason is very proud to be in the school play. How is he going to feel when he is torn between wanting to have both of his parents there to see him perform and knowing that if they do, there is going to be an embarrassing blowup?

• While the kid is visiting you, give him a weird haircut that Mom won't let him have, or let him get his ear pierced. You get the idea.

• Then there are all of the obvious things. Don't have the kids ready for visitation, don't show up for the scheduled visit saying, "I got held up at the office," cancel at the last minute, return them late, don't be there at the appointed time when the kids are returned . . .

• Prevent them from participating in their favorite activities because its "your" time.

It may be that being on the All Star team or being in the soccer playoff or dance recital is the most important thing in your kid's life right now. Kids can be notoriously self-centered and believe their universe will explode if they don't get to go to whatever special event is scheduled for a week from Saturday. If the week from Saturday happens to be "your time," the quickest way to alienate your kid is to refuse to give up "your time" and the "family outing" you planned so he can play in the All Star game. If you want guaranteed long-term resentment, this is a good recipe.

Parental Alienation

It is sad to say that there are some parents who will deliberately embark on a course of alienation designed to turn the children against the other parent. Much has been written in recent years about parental alienation syndrome. I am sorry to say that it is real. It is obvious, of course, that the parent who would deliberately alienate his child from the other parent does *not* care about the child. This is the ultimate power and control battle and has absolutely nothing to do with concern for the child's welfare.

I once refused to accept a case for a client who continually referred to her former husband (the father of her four-year-old) as

"Hitler." When I cautioned her that it was most damaging to the child to hear his father referred to in this way (even at his tender years), she assured me that she never used the term in front of the child. Frankly, it tripped so lightly off her tongue that I knew she was lying. Hitler was who she thought he was, Hitler was who she told everyone he was, and that was the definite message the child received. I am sure the four-year-old had no idea who Hitler was, but he knew it meant somebody bad.

Less extreme is the parent who, although not consciously trying to alienate the children, seeks to interfere with and restrict the amount of contact the children have with the other parent. Except in cases where there is a legitimate fear of physical or sexual abuse, this is indefensible. There is also a very practical reason not to do it; it tends to backfire.

Kids know when one parent does not want them to see the other. If their access is restricted, two things tend to happen. First, on the limited occasions when the noncustodial parent actually has the kids, he goes out of his way to make the visit fun and as memorable as possible for the kids ("Disneyland Dad" and "Marineland Mom"). Because the visits are so infrequent, he wants to make them as special as he can.

This gives the kids an unrealistic image of the parent. They tend to fantasize that life is always fun when the go to see Dad and Mom is the one who nags them to brush their teeth and do their homework. Frankly, if Mom wanted the kids to get a more realistic picture of who Dad is, she would make sure that he had some tooth brushing and homework time as well. This tends to end the fantasy very quickly. Unfortunately, however, many custodial parents don't see this. They are so afraid that the children will love the other parent more that they can't help consciously or unconsciously conveying the message that the other parent is bad.

A particularly malleable child might adopt the custodial parent's attitudes completely and we then expend into alienation. However, a child who thinks for himself is going to remember two things: First, the custodial parent yells at him all the time to do things he doesn't want to do (of which all children perceive their parents to be guilty), and second, the noncustodial parent always provides a good time so they can play and have fun.

So, if your spouse wants more time with the kids and we are not talking about true abuse, the best way to give the kid a dose of reality is to let her spend some "real world" time in the other parent's house. Let her stay long enough to acquire a few chores and restrictions there. You may be surprised to find out she appreciates you a great deal more when she comes back.

Before you engage in any of these games, think twice about your kids. It's perfectly natural to be angry with your ex. There may be lots of issues about which you feel quite justified in fighting. But don't make your kids witnesses, much less victims of those battles.

18

Leaning On the Kids, or He Who Leans On Short Crutches Gets a Sore Back and Strains the Crutches

Very few divorcing parents would consciously and deliberately add to their children's pain. However, all too often parents turn to their kids for emotional support.

This may start as a perfectly innocent way of reassuring the kids "We're all in this together." Even though one person has left the family circle, the rest of us are all interdependent and care about each other. It can unfortunately segue into the children becoming emotional and psychological props. These patterns are no less damaging because they are unconscious.

As with so may other issues raised in this book, this is one to be discussed with your therapist. My goal is simply to alert you to the danger and highlight the extreme and unfair burden it places on your children.

Whether it begins as circling the wagons in a time of mutual trauma and stress or for some other reason, don't get into a situation where your kids are taking care of you, either emotionally or physically. They have enough to deal with simply getting through the process themselves, and it is your responsibility to be the grownup.

You should not be discussing the divorce with your children and certainly should not be placing them in a position of choosing sides. I have had this discussion with many clients. Sometimes I get the response "Do you expect me to *lie* to my children?" In a manner of speaking, yes. If you consider it a lie to refrain from telling the children what a jerk you think the other parent is, then lie. I would prefer that you simply tell them the part of the truth that is healthy for them to hear; that is, that you love them, that the other parent loves them, and this has nothing to do with them, it is between Mom and Dad. That is not a lie. If you perceive that you are lying to them if you do not share the intimate details of how much you hate the other parent, so be it. I call it being a grownup and a caring parent.

As the adult, it is your responsibility to determine how much of the truth they are ready to hear. Depending on the age and maturity of your child, you can "dose" the truth. This means you should be guided by what the child wants to know (rather than by what you want to tell him). This in turn is determined by the child's interest and curiosity.

I don't care of your kid is 17½ and is practically grown up herself. Don't lean on her. A kid who becomes your caretaker during this trauma may be paying a high psychological price for years to come.

It won't help you, either. You will be substituting a dysfunctional parent/child relationship for a dysfunctional marital one, hardly the optimum way to promote your own journey to emotional health.

Don't by word or implication indicate to your children than they need to "stay home and take care of Mommy." I once saw a mother who kept the children home from school on days she felt particularly needy and would write that in the school excuse. This applies to visitation as well. It is OK to let your kid know that you are going to miss him when he goes to visit the other parent; it is not OK to make him feel that he should forego the visit and stay home to keep you from being lonely or make him feel guilty for wanting to go.

Finally, if your child asks you questions you don't feel you should answer, don't ever be afraid to say "I don't know" or "That is private and I would rather not talk about it." Children understand privacy, and expect it themselves. It is much safer to err on this side than to risk the psychological trauma which inevitably results from the over involvement of the children in the parents' conflict.

19

Custody
Evaluation

If you have gotten as far as having a custody dispute assigned to an evaluator, there are a number of things which you can expect.

First, a private evaluator will generally (but not always) have more time to spend with you, your spouse, and your kids than an evaluator provided by the court. Some counties have wonderful family court services or similar adjuncts. Others can do only a very limited intervention, and some are downright dreadful. Some are so overworked that the evaluation doesn't start for six to eight months after your separation. Frankly, an "evaluation" which doesn't even begin until the parties have been living in separate households for six or eight months is not much of an evaluation. You may not be able to afford a private evaluator, and as a result have little choice. However, if you can, and your county is heavily backed up and understaffed, I suggest that you seriously consider a private evaluator.

Whom should you select? First, you should probably defer to your attorney on this. Your attorney will (or should) know who is good in your area and be able to give you reasons based on personal experience. The individual should have a thorough grounding in child development. Most are psychologists, but many superb evaluators are also trained in social work (usually an M.S.W.) or as marriage, family and child counselors (M.F.C.C.). I would suggest that you not be overly concerned with the letters after an individual's name. The level of experience and the respect

WHAT ABOUT THE KIDS?

which their opinions are afforded by the local courts are infinitely more significant.

If your case is going to require psychological testing, that will have to be done by a psychologist. It can be accomplished either by the evaluator doing the testing himself (if he is qualified), or by appointing a separate psychologist to conduct the tests and report the results to the evaluator. I have found either approach to work perfectly well. The parents may or may not be tested psychologically. If they are, they will probably be given standardized tests such as the MMPI (Minnesota Multiphasic Personality Inventory), Rorschach, etc. Some evaluators routinely test the parents. Others believe testing should only be done when one or the other of the parties exhibits some indicia of mental illness. I have a personal bias against wholesale testing in the garden variety custody dispute, as I don't think the information added to the clinician's observations justifies the level of intrusiveness, but it is the evaluator's judgment call.

It doesn't make one whit of difference whether your evaluator is a man or a woman. Many of you will assume that a woman would tend to favor Mom and a man would tend to favor Dad. That has not been my experience. As with lawyers, it is most important to have the best possible person for your case, and I couldn't care less about the gender of the evaluator. I would, on the other hand, be interested in any demonstrated biases. I would reject an evaluator (as well as a judge) who was in the midst of a hotly contested custody fight himself. At the same time, I wouldn't arbitrarily reject someone because of a stated bias. For example, a very fine custody evaluator of my acquaintance is quite honest about the fact that he prefers joint custody. Now mind you, joint custody doesn't necessarily mean 50/50, but instead means that the children have frequent and continuing contact with both parents. Nevertheless, the same evaluator has on more than one occasion in my experience recommended not only sole custody to one parent, but no contact to the other, simply because the facts of the case were so egregious and contact with the parent was so damaging to the child. Therefore, I know that although he starts an evaluation with the assumption (and hope) that joint custody will work, I also know that he will make the hard decision if it is in the best interests of the child.

An additional consideration is whether your attorney has worked with the proposed evaluator before. This does not mean that someone she has worked with will favor her over the other attorney. However, your attorney will generally know how she likes to conduct her evaluations and can therefore better prepare you. Remember, the key is to get as much relevant information in the evaluator's hands as possible. There are any number of people to whom I regularly stipulate who have "recommended against me" in the past. I am more interested in whether the evaluator had good reasons for the conclusion he reached whether or not I happen to agree with those reasons, than whether he was so intimidated by me that he rolled over and played dead after finding out that I was in the case. If he'll roll over for me, he'll do the same for another attorney. Likewise, evaluators who routinely try to cut the baby in half so as to keep everybody "happy" (and as a result nobody is happy, least of all the kids) is equally unlikely to get repeat referrals from me.

Each evaluator is going to have his or her own style and preferred procedure. Some will want to start by meeting jointly with you and your spouse. Sometimes this is because they don't want either of you to feel that the other one "got the jump" by getting to him first. Certainly, I believe that any evaluator is going to want to see you and your spouse jointly at some point during the evaluation. Frankly, the interaction between the two of you when you are in the same room is going to be very different from your interaction with the evaluator when you meet individually. Since the joint interaction is what the kids are most likely to experience, and since many people go through major personality changes when they get in the same room with their ex, this is valuable information for the evaluator.

The evaluator will generally want to meet with each of you individually at least once and sometimes a series of times. Depending on the ages of the children, they may want to meet with the children individually and with each parent to see how the children interact with each parent. They may do a home visit in each household and may want to talk to day care providers and teachers. It generally is not helpful to give the evaluator a long list of your friends (a judge I know calls them "Friends of the Bride and Friends of the Groom") to attest to what a saint you are and what a jerk your spouse is.

Your attorney can tell you about the style of the evaluator who has been appointed for your case. Here are some general rules, however, which you would do well to consider:

- Experienced custody evaluators can smell a programmed kid a mile away.

These people have seen everything and if you think that you are going to score points by programming Johnny to say what you want him to say, think again. There are ways in which kids talk and there are ways in which adults talk, and it is very difficult for a programmed kid to be a natural.

- Evaluators are unlikely to ask your child to choose between the parents.

Doing so puts a tremendous burden on children and it is generally considered therapeutically unsound. Instead, the evaluator will be much more interested in the substance of your relationship with the kids than with whom the kid would prefer to live. For example, if your child spontaneously expresses a desire to live with Dad, they are going to want to know why. It makes a great difference if the reason is that the kid feels more comfortable with Dad than because Dad has promised him a car for his 16th birthday. They are much more inclined to want to know to whom the kid turns in a crisis and why. They are going to want to know what activities he does at your house and with the other parent. If one party tends to park the children with a babysitter or in front of a video whereas the other one actually spends time with them helping them do their homework, going on hikes and the like, that is going to make a difference. They may ask the kid who is more likely to help with the homework. If one parent sets all the boundaries and the other lets them run rampant out of guilt or in the hope that they will elect to live with the parent who lets them get away with murder, that is likely to come out in the evaluation too.

- The evaluator may or may not want to know why the marriage broke up.

If it is relevant to the kids, they may want to explore it. However, if it is clear that your agenda is to prove how unfit your spouse is because he elects to be unfit with someone else rather than with you, that isn't likely to score you many points. You will undoubtedly have a great deal of information you want to convey. Make sure that it is relevant to the kids and their needs and not simply venting how you've been wronged.

- Focus on the kids.

If you appear at the custody evaluator's office with an entire case prepared against your spouse demonstrating by chapter and verse what an unregenerate disgrace to the human race he is, you are unlikely to get the result you want. If, instead, you can illustrate through examples how his indifference to the children's needs has caused ongoing harm to them, you will be more likely to make your point. What matters to the evaluator are the children's attachments. A chronicle of your spouse's wrongs against you will do nothing more than waste the evaluator's valuable time on extraneous matters, leaving you less time to convey the information which is truly important.

- The evaluator needs to see who you are.

You are not being judged as an individual. What is being judged is the nature of the kids' attachments. You are who you are. If you don't think who you are is going to play well with the evaluator, this isn't the time to invent a whole new persona and try to convince the evaluator and the judge that it's real. It won't ring true. Instead, work on changing who you are into who you would like to be. You and your kids will benefit.

- When you go into a custody evaluation, prepare for it as carefully as you would for a trial. That's exactly what it is.

It is infinitely more difficult to set aside an unfavorable evaluation because you didn't get the proper information to the evaluator than it is to do it right the first time. Many clients have consulted me over the years for a second opinion on a "bad" evaluation. More often than not, they have a long list of information which "proves" the evaluator was wrong. Equally as frequently, they either didn't present the information in the first place because they were too busy castigating the other parent, or buried it in so much venom that they lacked credibility and the evaluator blew it off. Do yourself, your kids, and the evaluator a favor. Spend some time and thought on your childrens' attachments, their needs, and the ideal time sharing plan *before* you meet with the evaluator. Don't just wing it, assuming that of course you know what is right for your kids because, after all, you're the parent. Think about it. Consider what would be best for your children and be prepared to explain your reasons. Your thoughtful reasoning will pay off. The evaluator will thank you, and your children will thank you.

Here are some questions to ask yourself as you prepare for an evaluation:

- What are my children's special needs?

- How do Susie's needs differ from Matthew's?

- What are the special developmental issues in each child's life right now? Their most important activities?

- What are the most important issues the timeshare arrangement must meet for each of the children? Why?

- What is the ideal arrangement for these particular kids? Why?

- What important needs of the children are left unmet by the arrangement proposed by your spouse? Why? Why does your proposal work better *for them*?

- How do you anticipate the kids' needs changing over time? How would you propose to adjust the arrangement to address those changing needs?

When all else is done, remember one thing: If you believe in your heart of hearts that you are a *slightly* better parent than the other and it looks as though a custody fight is ensuing, consider carefully whether it would be in your childrens' best interests to leave them with the other parent subject to liberal visitation rather than to expose their bodies and psyches to a war. The children are going to be uncertain enough during your divorce. They don't need the additional apprehension of not knowing from day to day with whom they will live, where they will go to school and how often they can see their friends or the other parent. When I see a parent who will walk away from a custody fight for the good of the kids, while ensuring a lasting place in the kids' life and development, I know I've got a good parent as my client.

20

Blended
Families

In these days of serial monogamy, the issue of blended families is one which is inspiring countless graduate theses and keeping thousands of therapists in business. The therapeutic issues are far beyond the scope of this book. It is, however, important to address the practicalities.

The typical scenario goes like this: a couple is divorced. (H-1 and W-1). They have three children (C-1, C-2 and C-3) of whom they have joint custody. After the divorce, each remarries (H-1 marries W-2 and W-1 marries H-2). Perhaps W-2 and H-2 each have children (C-A and C-B go with W-2; C-X, C-Y and C-Z go with H-2). Sounds complicated, doesn't it? Wait till you try to arrange a visitation schedule that works for everyone.

If you think arranging visitation between W-1 and H-1 creates problems, you have no idea what the foregoing, quite common scenario presents in the way of complications. Is it better for each family to have weekends off while we coordinate the visitation weekends (i.e., everybody visits on the same weekend and everybody is away on the same weekend)? Or is it better to have each set of children have their own "quality time" with their own parent, that is, without stepchildren? If so, when do the parents get a break? What do you do with school vacations? You obviously have to start coordinating summer vacations in about February and what the hell do you do about the holidays? Unless both parties and the other two ex-spouses are all extraordinarily adult, cooperative and sensitive, you are going to have problems. How to you ensure that you alternate each kid's birthday and what on earth do you do about Mother's and Father's Days? Unless you are all quite civilized, soccer games are going to be hell and God help you at graduation.

The reality is you have chosen a new mate and that mate comes with baggage, a former spouse, some children, and a whole lot of history. If you love him that is part of the package, but it may not always be easy.

You may find that your little stepdarlings refuse to eat at your house because you don't make their favorite dishes as well as Mommy does. They may blame you for the breakup of their family. Then there are conflicts between the stepchildren in each family. All these possibilities come with the territory. There are therapists who build their entire practices around the problems of blended families. If you recognize your situation here, you might want to become extremely well acquainted with one of them.

In this situation, you will be well advised to practice flexibility and compromise; rigidity kills.

If you have a blended family, expect the normal scheduling problems of any family to increase logarithmically. How are you going to deal with coordinating visitation, lessons, soccer practice, back to school nights and the like? How are you going to deal with discipline? How does he feel about your disciplining his kid? What is going to happen the first time the kid says, "I don't have to do what you say; *you're* not my mother"?

Anyone who deals consistently with blended families will tell you that there is no single right answer. However, it is critical that you and your new mate talk honestly about how you are going to handle these issues and reach agreement with respect to each of your children. If either of you is perceived to show favoritism to your own children over the other's, be prepared for problems in the relationship. If neither of you can be flexible, you are in for a great deal of conflict.

Part IV

Support

21

Support, or "Which Bills Shall I Pay This Month?"

An interesting sign used to be prominently displayed in one of our local family courts. It read:

"NOTICE TO LITIGANTS: INSOLUBLE FINANCIAL PROBLEMS CANNOT BE RESOLVED BY THE COURT"

Unless you and your spouse are both fortunate enough to be highly paid professionals, support is likely to be an important issue in your divorce. If you have children, support is guaranteed to be significant.

There is more awful truth about support than just about any other area of divorce. Start with the economic reality that there is almost never enough money to go around in the first place. The pie is then split into two pieces, spreading it even more thinly. Add to that governmental tinkering with mandatory guidelines and the inevitable emotional overlays attendant to spousal support (or "alimony"), and there is more than enough ugly truth for just about everyone's taste.

Payors and recipients of support will never see eye-to-eye on these issues. I use the gender-neutral terms of "payor" and "recipient" advisedly. We are more frequently seeing fathers as custodial parents and high-income mothers who pay not only child but spousal support to their former mates. This so-called role reversal brings up all sorts of biases and stereotypes:

Incredulous successful woman client, after being told how much support she'll have to pay: "You mean I'll have to pay alimony to *him*?!"

Yes, indeed, dear. Didn't you remember this part when you were fighting for equal career opportunities and complaining about the "glass ceiling?" It goes with the territory. Speaking for myself, the trade off was well worth it.

I have had more clients go into shock over support than any other area of divorce. Not only are the issues financially difficult and legally complicated, they hit you right where you live. A support order can literally determine whether or not either party can live with dignity.

So, let's get started. Here are some of the truths that everyone needs to consider:

If there wasn't enough money for a single household, it's not going to be pretty when you try to stretch it over two.

American consumers quite consistently live beyond our means. Most middle-class American couples routinely spend every nickel they make and then some. Highly-paid "yuppies" raised this to an art form in the 1980s. With the poor, of course, it was rarely a choice; there never was enough money and it's not surprising that they face even worse poverty at divorce. What amazes me is the number of high income professionals who carry huge consumer debt with no immediate ability to pay it. For them, divorce sometimes means bankruptcy.

If you're the average, middle-class American family, you and your spouse have between you a house, two cars, a pension and some miscellaneous furniture. You may have an IRA or two, probably a couple of VISA accounts, several store credit cards and a home-improvement loan. You are barely managing the payments on the consumer debt and have little ability to reduce the principal. You probably have to scramble twice a year when your property taxes are due (if you are fortunate enough to own the house). When the kids need orthodontia, it's a real shock, and you haven't even begun to think about college expenses.

Then you separate. When you try to support two households on the same income and no longer have the economy of scale of a single mortgage, single utility bill, telephone bill, etc., there will not be enough money to go around. Something is going to give. The first to go are entertainment and vacations. Then the property taxes will go unpaid and, well, you see where I'm going. At this point, your attorney may be suggesting you consider bankruptcy to eliminate the debt burden.

The most important information for either a payor or a recipient at the beginning of the divorce is precise data regarding their cost of living. Your attorney will probably give you a questionnaire to complete, listing all your monthly expenses. She may caution you that most people substantially underestimate their expenditures. Accordingly, you should review a full year (or two) of check records and bills in order to obtain an accurate figure. Don't forget the credit card bills, because a large component of clothing and entertainment is frequently buried there, as well as Christmas and other gifts. If you can, compile this data before you go to see an attorney. If you're within average norms, you will probably be shocked at how much you really spend.

Your attorney will then tell you about the state guidelines in effect in your jurisdiction and most likely will run a computer program that projects a support figure based on the family income. This is going to be your second shock. If you are the recipient, you are going to immediately say, "But I can't live on that . . . " This is true; your bills are in fact much higher than the guideline support. It is also quite irrelevant.

As a recipient, you need to know that the court is not going to simply add up your bills, arrive at a grand total, add a component for the taxes, and tell your spouse to pay it. Unless you happen to be one of the very few super-rich, there will not be sufficient funds to pay the sum total of your bills and allow your spouse a reasonable living as well.

As a payor, you are not going to have a clue how you will live on what is left over, at least in the short term. (Lose 10 points if you say "Then *I'll* take the kids; I can raise them cheaper.")

You need to know that most courts have little discretion over child support, though there may be more latitude where spousal support is involved.

Whatever the mechanism by which the support is set, several things are likely to happen. First, the support may well be paid by wage assignment. If so, an earnings withholding order may be sent directly to your employer with instructions to cut a check to your spouse each time they pay you. Don't get all embarrassed. Wage assignments used to mean that you probably had defaulted in your support in the past and there was a pejorative connotation. That isn't the case anymore. In fact, many states make wage assignments mandatory. Employers hate it, but the legislature isn't going to lose much sleep over them. After all, enforcement of support orders is politically correct.

If you don't pay your support, the enforcement procedures are becoming ever more draconian. Tax intercept programs are proliferating, whereby a lien is imposed on your income tax refund, thereby "intercepting" the money and applying it to the support arrearage.

Many states now have licensing penalties as well. For example, if your work requires that you be licensed and that the license be periodically renewed, a notice of arrearage can be filed which will prevent renewal of your license until the arrearages are paid. This can also apply to driver's licenses. I'm not sure I understand the logic of this one too well. The presumption seems to be that the money to pay the arrearages does in fact exist, and if we turn the thumbscrews enough it will be produced. I'm sure that is true in many cases, but sometimes the money just isn't there, and this tactic isn't going to create it out of thin air. It obviously puts pressure on payors to raise the funds in the interim, but if they can't, where's the sense in putting them out of work? This is about as practical as throwing him in jail for nonpayment. Unless you're using jail to send a message or as a deterrent to defaulting on support, it really serves no useful purpose. If the payor is sitting in jail, he is not likely to be making money to apply to the support arrearages.

Years ago I had a client who was screaming at me to throw her husband in jail because he was paying partial (but not complete) support for her seven or eight children. The husband was a wage earner who clearly was trying to spread the money too thinly. I explained how jail wasn't a useful procedure for collection since he wouldn't have any money coming in, but she was adamant. When he was jailed, he of course missed the next support payment because he didn't get paid for the time he lost. I received an irate phone call from the same client, complaining that she hadn't been paid and demanding that I *do something about it!* Presumably she got the revenge she wanted by humiliating him, but it did her no good in the long run. It certainly didn't get her electric bill paid.

On the other hand, you might argue, "They can't get blood out of a turnip." True, they can't. But they can make sure the turnip doesn't have much of a life.

Truth: support is likely to leave everyone unhappy. Accept that fact and try to reach a compromise both of you can live with, however uncomfortably.

22

Support
Guidlines

When you first consult an attorney, you will probably be told that mandatory state guidelines for child support are now being imposed by the federal government, if not by the state legislatures. The formulas applied are steadily taking a larger and larger percentage of the payor's income, making for very unhappy payors.

The goal behind guidelines was to standardize support so that couples in similar financial circumstances obtained similar support orders. Guidelines have generally achieved that goal, albeit at the expense of the discretion to tailor an order to the specific needs of an individual family. If you are the recipient of support, your award is going to be very similar to the one received by anyone else who has the same incomes as you and your spouse. It may be totally unfair if you have significantly higher expenses that the norm, but the award may not take that into consideration. So be it. That is the price paid by individuals for overall consistency in support orders.

The final support figure may be based upon a computer program. You would be well advised to learn as much as you can about whatever guidelines or computer programs are used in your jurisdiction. Each of them varies slightly because they are based on different tax and input assumptions.

The underlying philosophy varies radically from state to state, although this issue is very much in flux as new federal mandates are being implemented. If you have the choice of filing for divorce in one of two or more jurisdictions, you would be wise to research the variations between them before making a decision.

There are, however, certain common denominators. Guidelines are generally driven by taxes and income. The computer will want to know how many children there are, with whom they primarily reside, and the incomes of both parents. It will then want to know about those expenses that are tax-related, such as mortgage interest. Generally, the computer will *not* make allowances for non-tax-related expenses such as utilities or consumer debt.

The computer will then apply the local guidelines and spit out a combination of child and spousal support or, occasionally, a "family support" figure, which lumps them both together for tax purposes. In some jurisdictions, the result will be mandatory with limited exceptions; in others, only the child support component will be mandatory. Some jurisdictions don't even have alimony guidelines. Others totally disregard the custodial parent's income, no matter how high it is or put a cap on support in high income cases.

There is an interesting twist in the relationship between tax and support in some of the computer programs. If you run the program without regard to your mortgage payment, you will get one number for support. If you then remember that you actually have $1,500 per month of tax-deductible mortgage interest and plug it in under the recipient's column, the support will go down. *"What?"* you shriek. *"I just added a bill that I have to pay and my support goes down?"* Precisely. This is because the mortgage interest is deductible, and therefore the computer will say you don't need as much money because you'll be deducting the mortgage interest and will pay less in taxes at the end of the year. *"But how do I pay my mortgage between now and next April 15?"* you ask. The computer sits there silently blinking at you.

After going through this drill with the prospective recipient of support, we begin a rather predictable exercise. First, my prospective client will tell me, *"But I can't live on that."* This is, of course, an eminently true statement. I then point out what is left for the payor and ask how a second household can be sustained on the remainder. One of two things happens at this point. Either I can tell by the stricken look on my client's face that the message has gotten through, or she laments *"But it's not fair . . . "* We're talking reality here, not fairness.

There's a popular myth that pops up repeatedly. Quite frequently my prospective client will ask, *"But there are four of us and only one of him, so shouldn't we get four-fifths and he get one-fifth?"* Nice try. The answer is no, since in the average middle-class family, the one-fifth left over would leave the payor living in his car (if he still could afford one). Also, though some payors may disagree, the court really does want to leave them with an incentive to go to work.

When the intact family was barely getting by on the available income, both separated households are likely to slip into poverty, at least initially, while the finances are being sorted out.

If you are fortunate enough to be at the very early stages of planning for a divorce, I strongly suggest that you minimize the nasty shocks of your first visit to your attorney by doing the following:

- Become intimately familiar with your family's cost of living and know precisely where the money comes from and where it goes.

- Identify all the assets and debts together with precise balances for each. Find out which debts are secured and unsecured and what other resources, such as CDs, savings accounts and IRAs might be utilized to liquidate the debt.

- To the extent you can, get your financial house in order before you split the sheet. If you're not worrying about how to pay the consumer debt, you will be much more likely to keep food on the table and a roof over each set of heads.

Questions to ask your lawyer

After having done your homework, consult with your lawyer.

Since support philosophies vary so radically from state to state, I cannot predict what is likely to happen in your case. I can, however, suggest some questions to ask your lawyer:

- Does your state have a support guideline? (They all should by now.)

- Are the guidelines mandatory or discretionary? If discretionary, what factors in your case would cause the support to deviate from the guideline?

- If mandatory, are there hardship or other mitigating factors which might allow the result to be varied?

- Does your state award spousal support or alimony?

- Is that part of the guideline?

- What are the factors which are used to calculate the guideline support? Do the courts consider income only, or are your expenses relevant? What information does your lawyer need in order to accurately estimate the guideline calculation?

- Does the guideline consider the recipient's income, or only the payor's?

- How do the guidelines treat children of prior or subsequent relationships? Are they considered at all?

- Are the spousal support guidelines treated the same as child support?

- Do the guidelines consider the new mate income of the payor? Of the recipient? If so, is all of the income considered, or only part of it? How do they treat stepchildren?

- Does your state expect custodial parents to work outside the home? Do the guidelines impute income to someone who is not working to capacity?

- Can you get child support for children in college?

- How often is support reviewed? Do the guidelines provide for cost of living adjustments? What is the standard used (e.g., Consumer Price Index)?

- Will the judge to whom your case is assigned be likely to depart from guidelines in cases such as yours?

- Is support ordinarily paid by wage assignment? How does this work?

- What if you object to the guideline amount? (Everyone will . . .)

- Is there a cap on support in high income cases in your state? What is it?

It is obvious that the end result can deviate dramatically depending on the answers to these and similar questions. Ask them, and be sure you get answers you can understand. If you have the ability to file in one of two or more states, investigate the guidelines in both states in order to make an informed decision.

$$23$$

Choices —
Part II

Your place in the support scheme is largely the result of choices you made years ago.

Every day of our lives, we are making choices. It's an absolute fact that the choices we make when we believe we're going to be married forever are different from the ones we would make in contemplation of separation and divorce.

At the time you had your family, you and your mate may have been utterly committed to the importance of the children having a full time parent. You may have followed up that philosophical commitment by giving up your schooling or career to stay at home with the children.

These decisions are going to have far-reaching impact. If you are the wage earner and chose, for the good of your children, to have a stay-at-home spouse for 7 or 10 or 15 years, that decision is going to have financial consequences. Now that you are separating, don't expect the parent who has been assisting in the kids' classrooms and schlepping them to soccer practice and lessons to suddenly become a brain surgeon or go out and earn 6 figures a year. Even if your spouse was a straight-A student in college and had a highly promising career prior to the birth of the first child, the choice to stay home for all those years means the training is stale. It's going to take time. And be fair. If it was OK with you for your wife to stay at home with the kids while the marriage was intact, my guess is that a judge is going to find it is OK for that same pattern to continue after the separation, at least for a while. You are going to pay support for now. Period.

If you're the one who opted to stay home with the kids and give up the promising career, I'm sure that at the time you made that decision you thought it was the best for yourself and your family. In most instances, that doesn't mean you are going to get so-called "lifetime" support (more about that later). The courts most likely are going to pressure you to pursue education or training consistent with your abilities, the job market and your children's needs.

Don't expect most family law judges to be overly impressed with the argument, "But I *can't* work; I have children." Elsewhere in this book I have advised individuals contemplating divorce to sit in a courtroom and watch the divorce calendar for a day or two. In no area is this more instructive than in the area of support.

Most judges handle dozens if not hundreds of cases every week. In most of these, the litigants don't have enough money to support one household, much less two. In the vast majority of cases, the family simply can't afford the luxury of one parent staying at home with the children. Except for the very poor, where public assistance is an option, and the very rich, where it isn't needed, most families require two incomes simply to get by. Working may well be an economic necessity. The judge may in fact share your philosophical belief that it is better for children to have a stay-at-home parent. Some states even codify this as a policy. The reality, however, is that in many American households, the money simply isn't there.

Don't overlook the possibility, also, that the judge herself has small children, children with whom she'd like to spend more time. When you say *"But I can't work; I have children,"* she's not likely to be moved by your arguments. She has kids and she works.

Suppose you are the bright, college-educated recipient of support, and suddenly find yourself forced to consider career and training opportunities. Don't waste your time railing against the gods for the failure of your expectations. Instead, take this opportunity to decide what you would really love to do, what is practical, considering your age, talents, education, and economic circumstances, and devise a plan for becoming as financially independent as you can. Do it for your own protection because you never can tell what is going to happen a few years down the road.

Be realistic. This isn't the time to say you always wanted to get a Ph.D. in art history so you could become a docent at the local museum.

But more about sensible career choices later . . .

The Myth of "Lifetime Support "

I have counseled countless clients to never use the term "lifetime support." They don't listen.

In most states, the courts recognize that in a "long-term marriage" (defined as anywhere from seven to 20 years in duration), one party may have foregone career opportunities in order to concentrate primarily on domestic duties. The courts recognize that those choices (and the choice was, of course, made by both parties to the contract) have resulted in a diminution of earning capacity. They will grant long-term support in such cases. In California, we refer to a spousal support order that continues "until death, remarriage or further order of the court." Those words do *not* mean for life. They mean just what they say, until somebody asks the court for a different support order and convinces the judge that a change is appropriate.

At some time in the future the payor is likely to file a motion with the court asking that support either be reduced or terminated. The courts may entertain motions requesting that they admonish the recipients of support on their duty to maximize their own earning potential and become as self-supporting as possible. So, after six or seven or eight years of spousal support, you may be hit with a motion to either reduce or terminate your support. You will then probably be utterly shocked because, of course, you thought you got "lifetime support." There is no such thing.

Assume that your spouse is going to ask that your support be reduced or eliminated at some point. If you have chosen to ignore that reality and "think about it tomorrow" a la Scarlett O'Hara, you will to be in for a nasty surprise.

There are long-term marriages where support does, indeed, last for a very long time. Even length of marriage, however, is no guarantee against future vicissitudes.

I have seen numerous hearings in which a couple was married for 30-35 years. The wife never worked outside the home and had absolutely no marketable job skills. When the husband retired, his income was reduced and he sought to have support modified as well. It is tragic to see the number of couples who have made no plan for that eventuality. Perhaps in the divorce, the wife decided it was important to her to keep the house, so she traded it for her interest in the pension. When retirement time arrives, the husband's income is reduced. He seeks a modification order which is granted because, of course, he now has less income. If she never considered the possibility, she may well lose the house because there was only enough retirement income to support one household. Too many people are being reduced to a poverty level at stages in their lives when they have limited options, simply by lack of prior planning.

If you have a so-called long-term marriage (and check with your attorney for the definition in your jurisdiction), and receive spousal support, do yourself a favor. Don't even think the words "lifetime support," much less use them in conversation. Recognize that support can always end, whether by court intervention or death or disability. Assume that sooner or later you may have to support yourself, in whole or in part, and plan for that eventuality.

As a footnote, I would suggest that you not respond the way one of my clients did to the foregoing speech. She was bright, talented and educated and had an enviable country club lifestyle. When I pointed out to her that even her highly-paid and guilt-ridden executive husband was likely to move for modification of support in the future, she said, "Well then, I'll just have to find another man to marry me."

There's a word for earning your living that way. And what happens when husband No. 2 loses his job, etc . . . ?

24

The Payor's
New House

Suppose that you are the payor of support. At the early stages of the divorce, you were probably living at a mere subsistence level. Too much money was coming out of your paycheck for you to live comfortably, but somehow you managed to keep body and soul together and move up in your job. The studies show that in the years immediately following divorce the high-income earner (i.e., payor) tends to recover much faster from the economic disaster of divorce than does the recipient. The recipient may be in the same house as during the marriage, but the standard of living tends not to improve.

Suppose that three or four years after the divorce you are now getting back on your feet financially. Perhaps you've even remarried and started a second family. Then the dreaded process server arrives at your door to serve you with an Order to Show Cause to appear on a given day and present your case why your support payment should not be increased. There are many nasty surprises awaiting you when you return to your divorce lawyer's office.

First, unless your divorce was very recent, support guidelines have changed radically. Moreover, your income has most likely increased significantly since the divorce. Therefore, even had the guideline formula remained unchanged, you would probably be facing an increase simply by reason of your new income.

However, you are most likely to be caught in a double bind. Not only has your income increased, but the support guidelines are taking an ever greater percentage of the available funds. The new schedules would take a much larger bite even if the income remained unchanged, and a higher amount yet if income increased.

After I've told you what the new support number is likely to be and revived you from your faint, several things will be happening.

By now, your new wife (who accompanied you on this visit for moral support) may be threatening to divorce you, because in some states new mate income is available for support, and she retches at the thought that her hard-earned income could help support *that woman*.

You may be thinking about the new house you just bought or the new boat that you won't be able to pay for if your support order is increased. Sorry. Most judges are not inclined to reduce guideline support by giving the boat a higher priority.

Don't expect to get very far with your argument that you now have a new family to support, so you can't afford to support the "old" family to the extent of the guideline order. You chose to have the first family and with full knowledge of your obligations to them you chose to have a second. Many support calculations will give you a deduction for the children of the new marriage, but the deduction rarely exceeds the amount of child support you are paying for children of the first family.

This is not the point to threaten a custody fight because it would be cheaper to raise them yourself than to pay the support to your ex. Instead, refer to Chapter 15, "Kids Aren't Jelly Jars" and lose 10 karma points.

Instead of railing against fate and the unfairness of it all, there are a few positive steps you can take.

Look carefully at your own spending habits. If you've bought a new house and a new boat and the kids go back from visitation with stories of all the toys at your place, don't be surprised if your ex-spouse files a motion for increased support. If your support order hasn't been modified in the last year, it is most likely behind your own income. Don't be angry at your ex for filing the motion; she probably has no economic choice in the matter.

Second, if you didn't do it at the time of the initial divorce, look at the practical suggestions for buying out the support rights or building work incentives into the support order (See Chapter 26, "Buy Outs and Employment Incentives").

Third, recognize that you are much better advised to periodically agree to cost-of-living adjustments in conformity with your increasing income (and, hopefully, the recipient's retraining efforts) without recourse to court. The adjustments that you and your spouse work out between you are likely to be more favorable than those that the courts would impose, and you save the attorneys' fees for fighting the modification. And if she does get remarried, send a nice wedding gift . . .

25

The Standard to Which I'd (Like to Have) Become Accustomed

Most states have provisions for spousal support or alimony tied in some manner to the marital standard of living. In practice, this isn't as significant as it may seem. Marital standard of living is frequently irrelevant because the income is never going to be sufficient to support two households at the standard once a split takes place. If you fit into this category, the following discussion is going to be largely academic. Moreover, unless you are fortunate enough to be married to a multimillionaire and there's money to burn, it is unlikely that the courts or the economy are going to recognize tennis at the club as a career.

The definition of marital standard of living is vague in the extreme. While most of us have a general idea of what it means ("I want to live as well after the divorce as I did before"), it is very hard to quantify.

Generally, the courts will look to subjective indicia of marital standards of living. What type of neighborhood did you live in? How many and what types of cars did you drive? How often were they replaced? How often did you go on vacation and where? Were the children in private schools? Did you belong to a country club? How often did you go out to dinner and where? How much did you spend? What bills were paid from an expense account or by the family business? Where did you generally shop for clothes? How much did you spend? Did you routinely save money as a family and if so, how much?

Whether you are the payor or recipient of support, these are the questions which you should be asking yourself. Document the answers to the extent you can, since the information is elusive and subjective at best and can quickly become stale. You will never have access to better information than you do at the time of your separation.

Ironically, the marital standard of living itself frequently doesn't become relevant until long after the divorce is over. Typically, at the initial separation there is insufficient money to support either of you at the marital standard. Therefore, the question was academic then and nobody bothered to gather and save the evidence. In most cases, it takes several years for the payor to recover financially from the economic shock of the divorce. He is making more money, and the recipient takes him back to court in order to get increased support based on the increased income. She then has a double burden. First, she has to prove that the initial support order was insufficient to sustain the marital standard of living. In order to do that, she must establish what the marital standard was and then she must prove that the current support order is insufficient to sustain it. By this time, evidence is gone and it is often almost impossible to reconstruct it.

In most cases, there is very little that you can do other than simply gather whatever information is available to you at the time of the divorce and hope that you will have what you need later to prove your case.

If you are a recipient, you need to preserve whatever evidence and documentation you have which will demonstrate that your current standard of living has deteriorated since the separation. Generally this is going to mean a detailed review of records of the last year or two of the intact family. You may never have an opportunity to use this information, since it only becomes relevant if the payor's income level rises high enough to justify an increase in support during a period when the court still has jurisdiction to modify it. However, since it is so difficult to reconstruct after the fact it is a good idea to simply assemble the information, whether or not you'll ever need it.

Payors should also do their homework at separation. When a court is called upon to make a support order, the parties are required to file a financial declaration of some kind demonstrating their income and living expenses. Different jurisdictions have different rules, but in California this is required to be on a Judicial Council form called Income and Expense Declaration. We have all seen them come in. The prospective recipient of support files a declaration under penalty of perjury which states that the essential family expenses exceed the family income by thousands of dollars per month. Sometimes this is in fact true when people have been living on credit cards. More frequently it is wishful thinking. When one of those inflated financial declarations is presented, the payor should review the actual family records and determine the true expenses by compiling and averaging them. The last thing you want is for an inflated declaration filed at the time of the initial separation to become the "standard" for a later hearing on modification of support just because it happens to be in the court file. This can occur if you simply dismiss it at the time it is filed as ludicrous on its face. The judge who will be making the decision on a modification hearing five or six years later has no way of knowing whether it is true or not. Accordingly, both sides need to do their homework on this issue, and neither can afford to simply dismiss the issue unless you know as a matter of fact and law that the court is only going to have limited jurisdiction in the future to modify or award spousal support.

Note also that the marital standard of living may be irrelevant when it comes to child support. In California, for example, the recipient who is seeking spousal support or alimony cannot receive support above the cap established by the marital standard of living.

Not so for children. If Dad's income goes through the roof after the separation, the children are entitled to ride the upper inflationary spiral of his income and enjoy the standard of living of the higher income spouse, regardless of whether it substantially exceeds the standard of living prior to the parents' separation.

Ask your attorney the precise meaning and interpretation of these issues in your jurisdiction and don't assume you don't have to put the evidence together now because this isn't going to come up until later.

The "Ball-Soxer"

My former legal secretary coined a phrase some years ago that I have always found amusing. One day she returned from lunch railing about "ball sox people." When I asked her what she meant, she said she was referring to a particular type — a woman who was married, educated, unemployed, had 2.3 children and drove a Volvo station wagon (nowadays a minivan or utility vehicle), played tennis three mornings a week and invariably showed up at the grocery store in her tennis outfit. My secretary had just been trying to make a quick trip to the store on her lunch hour and found long lines of "ball sox people," wearing little tennis dresses with their tennis socks, hence the term. Her complaint was that she, like everyone else who worked for a living, had only limited time to go to the store and run errands. In her view, "ball sox people" could go to the store any time they wanted all day long and it was unfair of them to create long lines during the lunch hour when working people were in a hurry.

This phrase stuck and spread through my office to describe a particular type of woman. She was generally married to a successful and highly paid executive. At the time she consulted me, the children were probably teenagers and she was relatively free of day-to-day and hour-to-hour parenting responsibilities. She finally had the free time to engage in the social activities she liked. She could meet friends for lunch and play tennis or golf and probably belonged to a country club.

When she came in for her initial consultation, her primary financial concern was generally that she wouldn't have to go to work.

I must confess that I can see her logic. Who in their right mind would not want that life? If I had it, I wouldn't want to give it up either. On the other hand, as someone who has always worked for a living, I have limited sympathy with the concept that she gets to retire at 38, and he has to work to 65. I said that very thing to one of these prospective clients on a day when my fuse was rather short. As you might imagine, this was a professional relationship that did not flourish.

It is going to be quite difficult to sell a court on the argument that an intelligent and able-bodied recipient of support should not have to do something to contribute to her own support. This is particularly true if she has been an active volunteer, organizing charity functions or running the local thrift shop. There are very few people who truly have no marketable skills or who, by reason of physical or emotional disabilities, are incapable of working. Additionally, most states require that both parents contribute to the support of their children to the extent of their abilities. It's not just a one way obligation.

And if you're divorcing a ball-soxer, stop complaining. She probably made a great corporate wife as you were moving up the ladder and it suited you to have her available while you were together. If you're honest, you'll probably admit that you didn't want her to work, as the demands of her job might have conflicted with the demands of your job or the kids. It worked for both of you while you were together, and you're going to pay for your decisions, at least while she updates her education and training.

26

Buy Outs and Employment Incentives

I am frequently asked about spousal support buy outs and encourage clients to consider them in appropriate cases.

A spousal support buy out occurs when the payor of support pays the recipient a lump sum of money in exchange for a permanent waiver of spousal support or alimony. Generally, this only works for spousal support and not for child support.

There are some rules you need to know if you are considering such an arrangement. First, few courts have the jurisdiction to order it over objection. You and your spouse can agree on a buy out and, if so, the courts will enforce your agreement. But they cannot impose such an order if someone objects.

If you are considering offering a buy out of support, don't just simply add up the number of monthly payments that you are likely to pay over the probable duration of the support order and assume you'll pay all of that up front. You certainly need to be able to estimate the probable amount of spousal support that would be ordered and the probable duration of the order. You need to factor in the likelihood that the recipient will become reemployed or remarried. You will also have to allow for the possibility that the payor will have significantly increased income during the likely duration of the support order.

Once all of these components are weighed, you should be able to estimate a range of predictable amount and duration for a support order. The next step is to reduce the total of your estimated monthly payments by an amount equal to the federal and state income taxes applicable to your jurisdiction. The reason for this is that spousal support paid "periodically," that is, on a monthly basis, is taxable to the recipient and deductible to the payor. Spousal support paid in a lump sum is not. Therefore, since it is tax-free to the recipient and not deductible to the payor, it should be discounted by the tax benefit. It is then discounted again for the present value of future dollars. The discount factor is always an estimate based upon current interest rates and market conditions. You can go to a CPA or a financial planner to do these calculations, or your attorney can probably give you a ballpark estimate, based on experience.

Recognize that these lump sum payments are always gambles on both sides. The payor is gambling that the recipient isn't going to get married quickly and therefore terminate the spousal support obligation before the projected duration. He is also gambling that his income is going to increase, and therefore he would be at risk for increased support payments. The recipient is gambling that she is going to be able to support herself from the lump sum plus interest and that her costs of living are not going to significantly increase.

Interestingly, in the mid-80s, we always assumed the payor's income was going to continually escalate and as a result, many high income payors were pushing buy outs. With the economic turn around of the late 80s and early 90s and the number of executives suddenly out of work, it now appears that the recipient made the better bargain in many of these cases.

There are some obvious advantages and disadvantages to support buy outs.

For payors:

They know precisely what they are obligated to do. They can make financial plans and know there won't be any nasty support increases in the future. They know that they can maximize their earning potential with absolute impunity (except as regards child support, of course) and needn't worry about the ex finding out about the big raise or the bonus. They don't have to pass up buying a house or a new car for fear the kids are going to tell the ex, who will then file a motion for more spousal support. Even if they have to borrow the money for the buy out, they are paying interest on a fixed term and know precisely when the obligation ends, as opposed to having an indefinite term and amount in an open ended support order. The longer the underlying marriage and the less economically self-sufficient the recipient is, the better the gamble is for the payor. The exception to this is if your ex is secretly planning to get married soon, in which case the support would end in any event.

For recipients:

They are in charge of their own finances and their own life. They are responsible for budgeting and investing. They needn't fear the ex suddenly losing his job or becoming disabled. If they are planning on getting married again or starting a lucrative new career in the relatively near future, this can be a very good gamble indeed.

In appropriate cases, I always encourage clients to consider a buy out, recognizing that it is always, but always, a roll of the dice for both parties. Fortunately, however, it is frequently a good one.

If you can't afford a complete buy out, consider some form of nonmodifiable support or employment incentives.

Most jurisdictions allow alimony to be treated as "nonmodifiable" in some respects. You and your spouse can agree to put restrictions, both as to amount and duration of alimony, which can give each of you important incentives.

Some of the possible restrictions are:

• Alimony will continue at a specific level for a fixed period of time and can be modified only in the event of the recipient's death or remarriage.

Such a restriction is designed to give the recipient an incentive to get a job. She can earn as much as possible without fearing that her alimony will be reduced based on her increasing income. The whole idea is that during the period of nonmodifiability, she has an incentive to maximize her earnings. The payor typically pays more than he normally would in exchange for the restriction. The trade off is that he knows exactly how much he is going to have to pay and for how long and can maximize his own income without fear of increased support payments.

- Alimony will not be modifiable unless the recipient earns more than a specified level of income.

Such an order is also designed to give the recipient an incentive to maximize her income. For example, if the vocational evaluation indicates that she can be expected to earn $1,500 per month and the payor wants to give her an incentive to do that, he may agree to an order which says that her support won't be reduced for a specified period of time unless she earns at least (for example) $2,000 per month. This means that she knows she can be employed for a while, building her career without having to worry about losing alimony. It enables her to get on her feet in a new job or industry and she develops a track record of employment which can be used in later modification proceedings. One would not want this type of order to go on indefinitely, however. It is important that it be either fixed for a finite period or, at the very least, set for a court review at a specific date in the future.

Again, in agreeing to such an order, the payor is gambling that the recipient will take the incentive, get into a job, and therefore, when he requests a hearing to modify the support downward, he will have evidence that the recipient can, in fact, earn money at a predictable level.

- Alimony will remain at a specific level for a fixed period of time and can be modified only if the payor's income exceeds X dollars or is less than Y dollars.

Such an order is designed to discourage interim modification hearings for relatively small variations in income. For example, if the parties really don't want to go back to court every year based upon the payor's cost of living and have to relitigate everyone's finances, they may establish a range within which they will agree not to go back to court. For example, if the payor's income is at $60,000 per year, they can agree that they will not go back to court unless his income exceeds $80,000 or falls to $40,000. Both parties take a risk here as the payor is going to have to pay more than state guideline support to get the restriction. He, of course, is gambling that his income is not going to go up more than $20,000 a year in a specified period and that he is not going to take a cut in pay. The recipient is getting a bit of a break on interim support in exchange for giving up her right to take him back to court over small incremental increases in his income. It is designed to reduce interim litigation and, again, give both parties some predictability in their income levels.

• Alimony will drop to specific levels at specific dates in the future (generally leading to an ultimate termination of support).

In a step down order, both parties are assuming that the recipient's re-employment and/or training plan is going to proceed according to schedule. It can be a risk for the recipient but as long as proper homework has been done (more about this in Chapter 27, "Vocational Evaluation") the risk can be minimized.

Finally, there are endless permutations of the foregoing restrictions which creative lawyers can build into support orders. You might have one type of support order for the first two years during the recipient's early retraining and then switch it to a step down or limited nonmodifiability. The goal here is to tailor the support provisions to the facts of your particular case in such a way that the risk to both parties is minimized.

In the proper case, you can have a support order which not only closely approximates the facts of life and the changes in your respective situations, but saves thousands of dollars in attorneys' fees which can then be apportioned between the parties.

27

Vocational Evaluation, or What Do I Want to Be When I Grow Up?

Many states provide for either mandatory or discretionary vocational testing for parties seeking spousal support. If you have been ordered to undergo vocational testing, don't panic. It can be an invaluable opportunity.

When I represent the recipient of support, I never force the other attorney to get a court order for testing. I will always agree, since I know the court will order it over my objection and it is a waste of legal fees to fight it. Also, I happen to think vocational counseling is a good thing. I generally suggest that my client beat the other side to the punch and start vocational testing and career planning without being asked. I'm fortunate to have one of the most competent career evaluators in the state practicing in my area. I will send my own clients to her without waiting to be asked.

There are several reasons for this. First, what can it hurt to know what you're good at? You may find that you finally have the opportunity to follow through on your aborted career plans, not only with official sanction, but at someone else's expense. Also, in these uncertain financial times, no one should assume that they can indefinitely rely on an outside source of support. To recipients, the evaluation process can be a real eye-opener. How exciting it is to find out you have aptitudes and abilities you didn't know about. And you might pick up some self esteem along the way.

Finally, if you are one of those individuals who, because of educational, physical or emotional problems truly can't ever be expected to be gainfully employed, you'll have a very competent witness in your corner. The vocational evaluator can testify to the precise conditions and circumstances which demonstrate your unemployability, thus relieving you of the onus of seeming to be dogging it.

My advice to payors of support is to get the vocational evaluation, and to the extent finances allow, support your spouse in training into a career.

There are countless resources. Excellent books about career choices abound, and most community colleges have reentry programs.

After you've identified something you're interested in, do your homework. Talk to people who are established in the career you are considering. Investigate opportunities in your area. How long will it take to complete your training? What programs are available locally? What do they cost? Is your prior training or education transferrable? How long will it take to get established once you've completed training? What do the jobs in that field pay? To start? With experience? What are the opportunities for advancement? Do the requirements of the career (travel, flexibility, hours, etc.) meet your needs?

Talk to people who are already working in the field you are considering. You will be surprised at how willing people are to answer honest questions if you tell them why you want to know.

Several years ago, court reporting was a hot "reentry" area. There were years where it seemed every woman client I had was being steered into court reporting. They had all seen fancy brochures from reporting schools, detailing how easy it was to become certified in a matter of months, and touting the vast sums to be earned on a part time basis with flexible hours. Now, I happened to know that court reporting is a very difficult career. It is physically and mentally taxing, and only a rare individual breezes through the training and certification process in the minimum time. I also knew there were good job opportunities for those who could. I talked to the reporter who takes all of my depositions and asked her if she would be willing to spend a few minutes with some of my clients telling them the facts of life about the business. My goal was not to dissuade them from an appealing career, but to be sure they were realistic about their goals and expectations of the rewards on the other end. She was quite helpful and gave my clients invaluable information. As a result, they made better decisions.

Be realistic. Your support order will likely be based on the career assumptions you make, so you had better be sure they are accurate. It is tragic indeed to find that you agreed to limited support based on false assumptions (or advertising brochures) because you didn't investigate the program. Just because somebody else became a hot shot realtor in three easy months doesn't mean that you will. Remember that you have other commitments, don't underestimate the time it will take, and don't waive future support based on unrealistic expectations.

Do your homework. If you need something to take your mind off the divorce and the emotional trauma after separation, I strongly suggest that the investigation and planning are good ways to occupy your time, and they will pay dividends in the future.

Retraining

Suppose you are a payor who can't raise the cash for a buy out, but you still have significant risk for long-range support. You have a long-term marriage and your spouse has limited marketable skills. There are some practical things you can to do minimize your long-term risks.

If you, as the payor, have risk for long-term support at more than a marginal level, I strongly suggest that you invest in your soon-to-be-ex wife's financial and business future and get her to invest with you. I do not recommend that you press her to go out and get the first low-paying, entry-level job she can find. This is particularly true if you have a good income yourself and are likely to get hit with a significant support order.

In a long-term marriage where the income is sufficient, I believe the payor is much better off striking a bargain to pay full (or even slightly higher) support for a fixed period now, in exchange for a termination of alimony thereafter, rather than to insist on an immediate reentry into a low-paying job.

In the typical case, the recipient of support is not employed. She (and generally, but not exclusively, it is she) has primary responsibility for the kids. If she's trying to go to school to develop marketable skills, deal with the kids and work at a part-time job, the stresses frequently become overwhelming. If something has to give, I guarantee you that what gives is going to be school. She probably can't afford to let the job go because her support was predicated upon her receiving that amount of income. She obviously can't put the kids on the back burner, and so the training simply doesn't happen. Therefore, she's left in a marginal job and never has quite enough income. Every time you have an increase in your pay or buy a new toy, she's probably going to be taking you back to court for more support. This doesn't mean that she's a terrible person; she probably has no financial choice in the matter.

On the other hand, if you can both bite the bullet for a reasonable period of retraining and pay her full support so that she doesn't have to work during the training period, she can focus on her studies. You would then have a date certain when the support would end, or at least step down to a much more reasonable level. In the long run, you wouldn't have to look over your shoulder, dreading the process server.

I must confess I have a much easier time selling this concept to recipients than payors, but I keep trying. Hope springs eternal.

Recipients have a different set of considerations. This is their opportunity to get the training they never had and I believe they should take advantage of it to become as self-supporting as they potentially can be.

There's an added psychological benefit to all of this. Once they reenter the job market and begin developing confidence in their abilities and pride in their work product, I have seen people who were profoundly depressed make major leaps in self-esteem. This is particularly dramatic if you had a spouse who told you, either verbally or in other ways, that you really weren't very bright and there wasn't much you could do that would be of value to anyone else. It's a great vindication to know that not only is there something you're good at, but someone is actually willing to pay you to do it.

On separation, payors generally try to pressure their spouses to take the first job available. I don't believe I have ever told a recipient to turn down a job or refuse to go to work in order to stick the ex with the maximum support order. What I have told them is not to get a dead-end job so that they are locked into that as their "career." Instead, they should consult a career counselor, look seriously at their aptitudes, abilities and the job market and come up with a realistic plan for training that the court (and hopefully their ex) can buy into. They will all be better off.

Above all, whether you are the recipient or payor of support, recognize that you are where you are because of choices you made. There were choices in the past that brought you to the point of being financially either dependent on someone else or responsible for someone else. There are also choices you can make from here on out that will either contribute to independence and self-sufficiency for both of you or keep you (as one of my colleagues has phrased it) "chained to the carcass of a dead marriage." Think about it.

Part V

Fear and Loathing, or Karma 101

28

The
Paramour

Many of you are reading this book not because made a conscious choice to divorce, but because you suddenly found out your spouse is having an affair. The existence of a "significant other" adds layers of complication to an otherwise relatively straightforward divorce.

First, let's get the emotional context straight. If you're the "leavee," you may be feeling hurt, rejection, abandonment, and humiliation. You may be fantasizing about hit-men. All of these feelings are perfectly natural as long as you don't act on them and instead deal with them in therapy.

If you are the "leavor," you may be feeling guilt, remorse and sadness, all tinged with the exhilaration of starting a new relationship. You, too, may need therapy to ensure that you don't give away the store out of guilt.

Each role presents unique problems. It is beyond the scope of this book (and the author's expertise) to tell you how to deal with the emotional issues in a therapeutic sense. It is important, however, that you keep emotional issues contained and not allow them to taint the other, relatively unrelated portions of the divorce process.

I always hear warning bells when a prospective client starts referring to her spouse's "paramour." The term is so loaded that I know from the beginning she is going to have difficulty in separating the emotional content from the financial and child issues.

Here are some things to do if you are the "leavee."

- Read *How to Survive the Loss of a Love* by Peter McWilliams, et al. Take it to heart, as it is one of the more constructive books I've seen in this field.

- Join a support group. If you can afford it, find the best therapist you can to address these issues in their proper setting.

Here are some things to avoid:

If your spouse met the new flame at work, resist the impulse to report it to management or otherwise stir up additional trouble at the office. In the first place, management almost certainly knows about the situation and is desperately trying to figure out how to handle it in such a way that the adverse impact on the office is minimized. Additionally, if you're dependent on support and your spouse loses a job because of your intervention, where does that leave you? I'm always amazed at the number of clients who have to be dissuaded from creating trouble at the office, as though they'll somehow benefit by getting their breadwinner (i.e. payor) fired.

Don't withhold the kids from the other parent as punishment for choosing to be with someone other than yourself. While it may feel good in the short term for you and the kids to circle the wagons against the common enemy of the new flame, in the long range the kids are going to suffer.

Don't take petty revenge on his or her personal property. I've seen some very creative stunts, all of which were amusing in the moment and ultimately counterproductive. I have seen people:

- Cut the zippers out of all his custom-made suits.

- Melt down her jewelry into one gorgeous glop of gold and platinum, studded by various indistinguishable gems.

- Throw his clothes in the driveway and repeatedly drive the Mercedes over them.

- Take his favorite book and methodically cut a heart out of each page before returning it to him.

All of these make great war stories in retrospect and are fun in the telling, but believe me, it's almost impossible to get the divorce back on track afterward. It's OK to fantasize about all of the foregoing and whatever else your fertile imagination may lead you to conjure up. It's not OK to act on your fantasies.

If you are the "leavor," you have a different set of problems. You are probably suffering from acute guilt. Remember that acute guilt, painful as it is, is infinitely preferable to terminal guilt. That occurs when you let your guilt feelings dictate your financial decisions. As with any of these issues, you will be best served by finding the best therapist you can and, if recommended, by getting into a support group.

Try to keep your divorce as separate as possible from your new relationship. How fair can it be to the new love of your life to have you constantly obsessing about how much you loathe the ex?

There's also a list of things for the "leavor" to avoid:

- Don't force your new lover down the kids' throats until they're ready.

In the urgency to get over the most painful part of the process, many parents announce to their kids that "now we have a new family." Forget it for now. The kids don't *want* a new Mom or a new Dad. They want the old ones to get back together and put an end to all this foolishness. Be sensitive to your children's needs and reactions, and if they are not ready to accept the new lover, plan on having some solo weekends with your kids. They will benefit and so will you, particularly if you haven't spent a great deal of one-on-one time with them in the past.

- Don't give away the store.

There are always certain parameters within which a divorce

settlement is relatively equitable. Parties suffering from the throes of guilt frequently give far more on support or property than they know they should. DON'T. If you are tempted to do so, put the property settlement on hold until you've had a chance to deal with the emotions and can make clear decisions. I guarantee that if you settle the case too quickly while you are still in "guilt" mode, you will resent yourself (for being such a chump) and your ex (for taking advantage) for the rest of your natural days.

A colleague of mine is fond of saying that "guilt has a very short half-life." That is eminently true. Give yourself the time to deal with your emotions properly before you allow them to dictate bad business decisions. I can assure you that the "wronged" party who is the recipient of the guilt-induced largesse is not going to feel any more forgiving of you if you overpay, and you are not going to buy the gold stars you want.

The nastiest divorces I have ever seen resulted from just this dynamic. The party in the position of financial power, in hopes of assuaging his own guilt or easing the transition for the other, pays far more support than the courts would call for. At some point, either because the guilt half-life has expired or the money has run out, a restructuring is required. In the meantime, the recipient has gotten used to the income and feels wronged all over again when it is reduced to a more appropriate level. You will never get any credit for having given too much too early. All you do is create false expectations. As a result, your probable next step is to become even more rigid and recalcitrant on the things you have not yet conceded in order to try to recoup what you perceive to be your loss.

Do yourself a favor and do it by the book, fairly, honestly and openly, but by the book from the beginning.

29

Mother Teresa and
Attila The Hun

A highly respected family law judge of my acquaintance has observed that in his many years on the bench, he has never seen Mother Teresa married to Attila the Hun. Now, I *have* seen Mother Teresa married to Attila as well as Lucretia Borgia married to St. Francis of Assisi, but I confess it is rare.

This is not to say that there are not truly abusive relationships and truly one-sided power struggles (remember, this book is addressed to the 90% or so of well-meaning couples who simply want to get on with their lives without being married to each other).

Recognizing that it takes two to make a divorce, just as it takes two to make a marriage, here are some approaches you might avoid:

Client to attorney:

"My wife is an unfit mother/drug addict/alcoholic, so she shouldn't have custody."

If she has been routinely caring for the children for years with your approval, don't expect a great deal of sympathy here, except in rare circumstances, especially if there's more than one child. If there is only one, and after the birth of that child you realized she wasn't cut out to be a parent, so be it. But if you then had more children with her, or left the one child in her primary care, what does that say about you as a parent? Either you were too stupid or dense to realize your kid was in danger, or you realized it but didn't care enough to intervene while it was convenient to you to have your wife provide child care. What is your excuse? And how well do you expect it to play with an experienced family law judge? Was she suddenly taken unfit after the first, second or third child? It is unlikely that she became an inadequate parent overnight simply because you decided to get a divorce.

"My husband is so violent. He should only see the children on alternate weekends."

or

"I'm afraid my husband is going to molest the children, so he should only have them one overnight a week."

I'm not moved. If he is so violent that he can't control himself, why did you have children with him? Where is the logic that says he's only violent on week nights, so weekends are OK, but week nights are not. If you say it is fine for your children to be with their father 20% of the time, but not the 35% he's requesting because he is *so* violent, the court is going to wonder how you know which 15% is the violent time. The judge is going to assume (correctly) that you want some weekend time free to pursue your own social life but otherwise deprive him of the kids, and violence isn't really the issue.

If you have real evidence of molestation, visitation should be supervised. If you're willing to let the kids stay overnight with him at all, you are either not very concerned about their welfare, or you are using the implied suspicion as an ill-considered weapon in the custody fight. Either way, you have no credibility.

Here's another cautionary note. Research has shown that allegations of sexual abuse which arise out of custody disputes are false in as many as 85% of the cases. Don't *ever* make such an allegation for tactical reasons. You are guaranteed the Divorce from Hell if you do.

"My husband is so crooked . . . I don't want to use this unless we have to, but he's been filing fraudulent tax returns for ten years."

Lose 10 points.

Don't expect sympathy if you willingly signed the tax returns and looked the other way during all the years the filthy lucre was illegally flowing into the family coffers. He didn't suddenly become a criminal just because he's now spending the money on somebody else. It suited you to have the extra income as long as you were the beneficiary. Moral indignation and righteous outrage are very poor form under these circumstances. Also, if you signed the tax return, you may be an accessory to the crime.

If he truly has been engaging in tax fraud for the last 20 years and you have "the goods" on him because you were aware of every detail, what does that say about your own morals? Why did you sign the tax return? I have asked this question of many clients. Their usual response is, "I had no choice," or "He made me do it." Nonsense. Most of the time, the client who offers to "come forward with the goods," is operating out of the same larceny as the ex. What she really wants is to use the information to get a better deal for herself. I think it is called "blackmail," a crime in most states . . .

I must confess I take considerable pleasure in pointing out to these people that if they signed the joint tax return knowing the existence of fraud, they became guilty of criminal acts themselves.

Suppose you are fantasizing about the withering cross examination your attorney will subject him to when he pulls out the fraudulent tax return. Don't be surprised to have the friendly I.R.S. agent come knocking on your door. Your hearing and case file are open to the public. Moreover, many judges consider themselves required by law to report instances of tax fraud when they surface in the course of a marital dissolution. The bailiff might decide to turn you in himself to snag the reward. This cross examination might just land you and your spouse in tax court, or worse, charged criminally with tax evasion.

I know of very few cases where someone was physically restrained while being forced to unwillingly sign a fraudulent tax return. If you signed the return knowing it was fraudulent, you made a *choice* to do so, however reluctantly. You may have found the alternatives (such as blowing the whistle on your spouse or precipitating an argument) unpleasant, but they were alternatives nonetheless. It may have bothered you to do it, but you obviously weren't distressed enough to make an issue of it.

And if you knew he was forging your name, why didn't you do something about it? You have the same legal obligation to file an accurate tax return as any other taxpayer.

"I know he's hiding money on me and I know how he's doing it, because he did it while we were living together during his last divorce"

Query: If he cheated his first wife financially as he was divorcing her, what on earth made you think he wouldn't do the same to you?

I know that in the first throes of love, we all think this is the relationship to end all relationships. Moreover, if the soon-to-be ex is making your lives a living hell, it is easy to unite against a common enemy and collaborate in minimizing income, hiding assets, etc. But don't kid yourself that the person who would do this *for* you would not do it *to* you.

I recognize that divorce frequently brings up anger and bitterness. At a time when you can't stand being in the same room with the other person, those character traits that in the past were merely irritating become wholly intolerable. However, as you are expounding on the fact that the man with whom you shared many years and several children is without a single redeeming quality, imagine the impact on your listener. Your attorney will not be the only one who wonders why, if he is so terrible, you stayed with him all of those years and why you chose *him* as the father of your children.

Hearing this diatribe, most people will (quite correctly) interpret it as hurt feelings and rejection. While some people do spontaneously change their characters (the proverbial mid-life crisis, which is blamed for more ills than toxic waste) your spouse is the person to whom you were powerfully attracted at one time. He didn't overnight become a different person. If he is an insensitive, devious jerk, he probably had all those charming traits before. What changed is not his fundamental character but the fact that you just found out about his secretary.

Ask yourself, as you are trashing the character, morals and probable parentage of your spouse, what does that say about your judgment?

So think twice before you publicly vilify your former mate. And, even if everything you're saying is absolutely true, remember one more thing. This person is and will always remain the parent of your children and the children don't need to hear it first, second or fourth hand. Every kid is entitled to believe that Mom is Donna Reed and Dad is Ozzie Nelson, and neither parent has the right to take that away.

30

Threats and Ultimata

In any emotionally charged situation, we are all tempted to say things we shouldn't. Whether you are on the giving or receiving end, avoid the following buzz words. Alarm bells should go off if you find yourself either saying or hearing any of these:

- *"I'll be fair with you as long as you don't see a lawyer"*

Say *what* . . . ? If you don't see a lawyer and discover your legal rights, how would you ever know if the proposal you're being given is fair? It is axiomatic that when you and your spouse are in the process of separating your finances and your property, your interests are no longer the same. Why on earth would you allow the person who is divorcing you and who would directly benefit from your loss to be the sole arbiter of what you are entitled to?

- *"If you leave me, you'll never see the children again"*

See Chapter 15, "Kids Aren't Jelly Jars". For reasons more specifically outlined there, any parent who holds the kids ransom out of revenge should lose custody. More subtle, but equally damaging variations on the foregoing are, "the kids will hate you for this," or, "If you insist on leaving us, the kids are going to be so devastated, they'll probably end up on drugs and it will all be your fault."

• *"I can't stand living in limbo. It's either her or me. Choose right now!"*

I seem to spend a great deal of my time dissuading people who don't really want a divorce from giving this ultimatum. Never, *NEVER* give your spouse an ultimatum that you are not prepared to have him accept. It only gives the fence-sitting spouse the permission he has been looking for all along. He can then shift the guilt and blame *you* for forcing the issue. Believe me, I know how hard it is to live in limbo, not knowing whether your marriage is ever going to be the same again, or even *be* again. Waiting for the other shoe to drop is torture. You feel utterly powerless and have no control over your own future. You are probably saying, "I don't care what happens; I can't stand this uncertainty." That's not a reason to force a divorce you don't want. I have frequently told clients that although it has been years since I read my Baltimore catechism, my recollection is that as bad as limbo is, hell is worse. Before you give an ultimatum, be sure you're prepared to accept either answer.

• *"I want to file for divorce to show him that I'm really serious this time"*

I also seem to spend a lot of time talking people who don't want divorces out of filing papers just to make a statement. In my opinion, the only reason to file for divorce is that you affirmatively want a divorce, not because you want to send a message, not because you can't stand being in limbo anymore, and certainly not because your friends are badgering you into it ("How can you put up with that? *I* never would"). If divorce is inevitable, you have the rest of your life to do it. However, once that paper is filed, a public record is created for all the world to see, a die has been cast. If anyone tells you that it is as easy to dismiss an existing divorce as it is to refrain from filing it, they are wrong. More often than not, the divorce develops a life of its own. People then get polarized into saving face, etc. This is not to say that couples can't reconcile after they have filed for divorce, but it is much harder than simply putting things on hold until you're each sure of your feelings.

31

How to Be Inducted Into the Jerk Hall of Fame and Lose 10 Karma Points

- Hold the baby pictures ransom and refuse to share.

- Fight for furniture that was long in your spouse's family on the theory that it was "a gift to both of us."

- Claim that the jewelry you gave your spouse for birthdays and anniversaries is "an investment" and should be divided between you.

- "Forget" to give your kid the phone messages, cards, letters and (yes, it does happen) gifts from the other parent.

- Fail to show up for visitation.

- Fail to return the kids from visitation.

- Hide money or run up the credit cards in anticipation of separation.

- Tell your kids you can't afford to buy them anything because the other parent "has all the money."

- Tell your kids you can't afford to buy them anything because "your Dad didn't pay the child support."

- Withhold visitation if the support is late.

- Refuse to let the kids see the other parent because she's "living in sin."

- When the kids come back from visitation, pump them as to your spouse's living arrangements, purchases, friends and social activities. Better yet, make them feel guilty if they don't voluntarily report to you.

- Make your kids choose between parents.

- Send only old, torn or ill-fitting clothes with your kids on visitation. Or, better yet, don't return the clothes at the end of visitation. Or, return the kids dirty, sick and hungry. Or don't let the kids take their favorite toy on the visit . . . you get my drift.

- Drag your children into court so they can see for themselves what a jerk the other parent is.

32

Pots and Pans

Fights about pots and pans *never* are. Instead, they're about power and control, hurt and rejection, unfulfilled expectations and sometimes, guilt.

Elsewhere I have offered suggestions for practical ways to divide furniture. Here, I want to talk about the dynamic that makes the division of personal possessions one of the most volatile issues in any divorce.

I have seen this reach epic proportions when the parties (who could easily afford their $30,000 per month mortgage payment) went to the mat over a single chair that could be replaced in any furniture showroom. I have seen multimillionaires fight over $500 worth of everyday china. Why?

Usually it's an issue of power. "I don't really want the glass-topped table, but I know that you do and so by insisting on having it, I win the power game." Or, perhaps, "If you make the last concession then that means I won." I have seen people fight for months and spend thousands of dollars in legal fees to obtain furniture they then donate to Goodwill. Anyone looking for monetary logic will be doomed to disappointment; psychological logic, now there's a different story.

Pots and pans, lamps and sofas are almost always symbolic of something else.

I used to be surprised at the frequency with which the very item that caused the most marital strife became the single thing that both parties absolutely *had* to have. Suppose that on a trip to an antique dealer, a couple found a particularly colorful and expensive area rug. She insisted she absolutely had to have it. He hated the very sight of it, felt they were being overcharged and only reluctantly agreed to buy it. For years thereafter, every time they got into an argument, he reminded her that she was the one who had insisted on purchasing that hideous rug, thereby subjecting him to the sight of it as a constant reminder of how he *always* gave in to her and she *always* got her way. Why should we be surprised that when we get the list of the furniture he wants, that very rug is at the top?

Dining room tables are another interesting psychological study. I have found the dining room set to be much more emotionally charged than the bedroom set, particularly in long-term marriages. It took me years to figure out why. However, for couples who were married in modest circumstances in the 1940s, 1950s and early 1960s, they generally had to wait years for their first starter house. In those days, most houses were not built with formal dining rooms. Therefore, achieving the house with the formal dining room and the furniture to go in it were symbols of success, of finally having "arrived." The dining room was probably the last major item of furniture purchased.

This hit me once when I was trying to talk a client out of paying her husband at least three times the value of the dining room set just to keep it from falling into his hands. He was gleefully extorting the cash from her because he knew she would never give up on the table. I demanded to know why she was insisting on making such an obviously unbusinesslike decision. She could easily replace the damn table for less than she was paying her husband. That's when she said, "*That woman* will never sit at my table." In her mind, she had worked, struggled and sacrificed for many years to finally achieve this symbol of success. The new woman was never going to play hostess at that table, and she didn't care what it cost her.

All of us have items of personal property in which we are particularly invested. Hopefully, you and your spouse will have very few pieces to which you are equally attached. There are, in fact, unique, one-of-a-kind pieces that can never be replicated. If you and your spouse are not fortunate enough to have two such unique pieces of approximately equal value, you may have a real dilemma. However, uniqueness is not a prerequisite to this problem. I remember once settling a case in which we had resolved every issue, including disposition of the house, the cars, the pension plan, various investment accounts and all of the furniture with the exception of a single vacuum cleaner. *Vacuum* cleaner? Excuse me, but where is the logic in this? It is not as though Hoover has gone out of business. It ultimately became quite clear to the other attorney and myself that neither of our clients was going to make the last concession. In order to get the case settled, the other attorney (a veteran of the family law wars) suggested that he and I each agree to pay for half the cost of a new vacuum cleaner so that we could all go home.

If you find yourself getting hung up on pots and pans, take a deep breath, step back and try to get a perspective on what it is you are really fighting about. If it is truly a unique and irreplaceable piece, God bless. If not, I suggest you adopt one of the methods outlined in Chapter 38, "Reasonable Solutions to Problems that Come Up in Every Divorce" for reaching an equitable division without consuming the cost of replacement in attorneys' fees.

A note about valuation here: Sometimes it will be necessary to actually have someone come in and appraise the contents of your house. I'd like to offer a few words of caution.

In the first place, 10 to 20-year-old furniture is going to have substantially depreciated in value unless it consists of antiques, oriental carpets and artwork and the like. This is particularly true if children have been playing Ninja turtles over, under and around it. If you're the one moving out of the house, please recognize that fact. Don't wrap yourself in an air of sanctimonious generosity and say, "I would never want to deprive you and the children of the furniture," and then claim it is worth $50,000. It probably isn't. Check with your attorney for the rules pertaining in your jurisdiction. In most cases, the court will look neither to the original cost of the item nor the replacement value. Instead, the court will consider what the furniture would bring today, *as is*, on the used furniture market. Imagine what you would get for the contents of your house if you were to put an ad in the local newspaper and have a garage sale next Sunday.

Take a long, hard look before you get into a war over who gets the family room sofa.

33

The Paranoia Factor

You're scared. Terrified. The person who is about to sit across a courtroom from you knows you better than anyone in the world. You have shared a bed with her for 14 years and told her every intimate secret of your heart. She knows where the old wounds are, the wounds which have never healed. He knows the thing that you fear most in the world and could use it against you if he chose.

Is that paranoia? I would call it legitimate fear. The problem arises when fear drives your judgment.

Anyone is vulnerable when an intimate relationship turns adversarial. That's of course the whole point of intimacy. If you weren't vulnerable, it wasn't very intimate.

So, what do you do? In this situation, fear is legitimate. The problem is that fear creates more unnecessarily nasty divorces than anything else, including infidelity.

Here is the scenario. You and your spouse, both reasonably intelligent, conscientious and well-meaning people, have agreed that you simply cannot live together anymore. You must separate. One night after the kids go to bed, you sit at the kitchen table and have the hard discussion. Who is going to move where, how are the bills going to get paid, how are we going to tell the kids, and the like. There is nothing more gut-wrenching than this discussion.

You both agree that for the sake of the kids, each other and the years you had together, you want it to be fair and amicable. You want to remain friends. Maybe you even agree to use the same attorney until you find out that simply isn't practical. Perhaps you both cry. Certainly in that moment, you both mean everything you say.

Everything goes along fine for a while, and then in a few weeks, one of you cancels the credit cards. The other one cleans out a bank account or diverts mail to the office. Whoever took the initial step undoubtedly viewed it as defensive, probably egged on by previously divorced friends or perhaps on advice of counsel. The other party is then made to feel like a chump for having trusted that moment of sincerity over the kitchen table, and battle is joined. Believe me, once the brawl commences, it will take six months, minimum, to get this process back where it should have been, if it can be done at all.

If you and your spouse have had, or are capable of having that conversation around the kitchen table, what can you do to see that the situation doesn't deteriorate?

First, make a vow to each other and to yourselves that you will do nothing, repeat *nothing*, to polarize the situation. Whichever of you is in the house and receiving mail will open it and make duplicates of every item, no matter how minor, and promptly forward them to the other. Trust me. The cost of photocopying is cheap in comparison with the cost of attorneys' fees.

You agree to meet, on neutral turf if necessary, to talk about the day-to-day problems: How can we get the bills paid in the interim? How do we pay down the credit cards? Who is going to use which cards and for what purposes? How are those bills going to be allocated between us? Which of the kids' expenses are we going to share? Where are we going to cut expenses?

The first one who violates the rules commits an act of war.

I am not saying that you should go blithely along like Pollyanna, leaving your financial future in the hands of the person who is divorcing you. By no means. The rules need to be clear at the outset. You will share every, absolutely every, bit of financial data with one another. The first one of you who is caught withholding is responsible for the fight. Make that clear. I don't think it would hurt to even write up a contract between the two of you detailing how you will behave with each other in the interim. If you are capable of trusting one another enough to do what I am suggesting, you can put it on paper and you can each take a copy of it. The rules would go something like this:

- I promise that I will share with you every bit of financial data available to me, including incoming mail as it arrives.

- I promise that we will jointly discuss how best to approach our children, and we will tell them about the divorce together. To the extent that it is possible, we will present a united front with the common goal of convincing our children that we both love them and we are divorcing not them but one another.

- We will work in good faith with one another to try to allocate our present debt and control the amount of new debt that we are creating during this transitional period.

- Our goal is to come through this in such a way that we can dance together at our daughter's wedding (see Part VII, "Post Mortem"), and we will each give our respective counsel and advisors instructions designed to accomplish that goal.

- We will put our children's best interests ahead of our own and make certain, to the extent that it is possible, that they do not suffer in the course that we are taking.

If you can do this, you get a gold star. Moreover, your children will bless you.

You *will* feel fear. There will be times when you realize how much this person knows about you and how devastating it would be if he chose to use it against you. You are indeed vulnerable. So is he.

Ugly divorces result from a violation of these rules. Somebody did something which they perceived as defensive and the other perceived as aggressive. Recognize that your spouse is feeling as vulnerable as you are. What may seem perfectly logical and reasonable to you may play as an indefensible act of war on the other side. It may make perfect sense to cancel the credit cards since neither of you can afford to incur additional credit. Perhaps you have already agreed that you need to put a curb on future bills. I guarantee you that if you cancel the credit cards without notice, however, you will be in for war.

Recognize, too, that when your friends are all telling you what you "should" do in order to "protect yourself," their advice may be perfectly valid. All I'm suggesting is that you and your spouse make a vow that neither one of you will make the first hostile move. If one of you violates it, so be it. If neither of you does, what a great thing that would be. It seems to me that it is at least worth a try.

Then be vigilant. Don't be stupid, but keep your eyes open for a violation of the rules.

I will even go one step further. If you catch your spouse in what you believe to be a violation of the rules, this is a time to confront. Ask why it happened. Your spouse may in fact be quite chagrined to hear that what he thought was simply a "housekeeping" move is perceived as a hostile act. Decide your subsequent course accordingly.

Don't ascribe the worst possible motives and don't be foolish enough to assume that your spouse is going to be looking out for your best interests. Keep your eyes, as well as your options, open, and you will be less likely to suffer through the Divorce from Hell.

34

The Dreaded
Prenuptial Agreement

"There must be a loophole — there's always a loophole"
Lucy VanPelt

Many of you signed either prenuptial or postnuptial agreements. Typically these are negotiated as part of a second marriage when one or both of the parties has already been burned by one divorce and wants to make sure that the assets acquired in divorce No. 1 are preserved for the children of marriage No. 1 and are not then redivided in divorce No. 2. Philosophically, this is quite understandable.

The problem arises when the prenuptial agreement goes beyond that, i.e., not only does it say that the assets brought into the marriage will remain separate until our galaxy becomes a black hole, but also provides that no way, no where, no how can there be any future joint property of the new marriage.

I have drafted countless prenuptial and postnuptial agreements. I have even drafted many of the "no way, no how" variety. My personal opinion is that (except in true cases of duress, as I will discuss later) anyone who signs the latter gets what they deserve.

Now, I realize that many of you were presented with such agreements after the wedding invitations had been mailed or even on the church steps before the wedding. Sometimes the agreement was accompanied with the threat that, "If you don't sign it, we don't get married." I understand that if the wedding has been planned and the invitations are out, the threat (overt or implied) of "no agreement, no wedding" carries inherent duress. No one wants to be humiliated in front of family and friends, particularly when the very person who is demanding that she sign the agreement is also saying "Don't worry, dear; I'll take care of you." *Of course* you want to believe it. After all, you are about to marry the guy. I have seen prenuptial agreements which were presented literally in the car outside the courthouse at Reno as the couple was about to obtain the marriage license. I contend that by definition, such agreements are obtained by duress, as there is no possibility of meaningful legal advice. I also believe that most courts will recognize duress in that situation. Mind you, I say most courts. If your agreement was obtained in that way, a judge may agree that the circumstances were unfair. However you cannot, repeat CANNOT, assume that is going to happen.

Good lawyers will carefully draft prenuptial agreements to cover several bases. First, they will make sure that the agreement is signed far enough in advance of the planned nuptials that there is no obvious presumption of duress. Moreover, they will insist that both sides have the agreement reviewed by independent counsel. More and more frequently, the attorney for each side is required to sign a certification which verifies that the attorney has explained all of the terms to his or her respective client and believes that the client understands not only the practical, but the legal consequences of the agreement. I frequently serve as the reviewing attorney, advising the client on the legal and practical impact of an agreement which has been drafted by an attorney representing the other side. Generally, the party asking for the agreement is the prospective groom, but it is more accurate to say that the party with the greater risk in terms of income and property is going to be more invested in obtaining such an agreement.

In most jurisdictions, prenuptial agreements are perfectly valid as long as they are properly done. I like to see them signed well in advance of the wedding, preferably before the date is set. I like to have two attorneys involved in the negotiation throughout the various drafts of the agreement and not just at the final review, and I want an attorney certification so that I know someone has explained to the other side all the legal consequences of signing.

All that being said, the person signing the agreement has the ultimate responsibility for its content. I have reviewed hundreds of these things. I could not count the number of times I have explained in thorough and very practical detail all of the reasons why my client should *not* sign the obviously unfair and one-sided agreement which has been presented to me for review. More often than not, I am met with a blank stare and the protest, "But I *love* him!" That, of course, is patently true. However, that doesn't mean you should sign the damn agreement.

Equally as frequently, someone will consult me about a prospective divorce. Somewhat sheepishly, midway through the initial interview, and after I have explained her property rights, she will venture, "Well, there is a slight complication; there is this agreement . . . " It turns out that I have just spent 45 minutes explaining all of the property rights which were waived by the agreement which the client has only now revealed.

Guess what . . . unless this is one of those gems which was executed on the courthouse steps or in the limo outside the church while the family and friends are all waiting for the first notes of Lohengrin, you're out of luck.

I invariably ask such a client whether she saw counsel before signing the agreement. More often than not, the answer is yes, she did. When I ask her what her attorney told her, she'll say "Oh, he told me not to sign it." I'm sorry. He *told* you not to sign it. You signed it anyway. Whose fault is that, and what do you expect me to do about it?

More of the bad news is that these agreements are very difficult to set aside. If your agreement is a post marital agreement (that is, signed after you were married rather than before), it is going to be even harder to set aside. In that case, you won't even have the implied duress of, "If you don't sign, we don't get married." You are already married, and you signed it anyway.

Believe me, I know that it is uncomfortable to feel you need to get legal advice to protect yourself against the person you are either contemplating marrying or already married to. It is awkward, embarrassing, all of those dreadful things. It is also necessary. If you signed an agreement either without legal advice (because you didn't want to make waves) or ignoring the legal advice you got ("You're crazy if you sign it"), you have a problem, and it is entirely of your own making.

I am frequently tempted to ask the clients what they thought they were signing. If they really didn't think it was important and they didn't think it was going to hold up in court, why on earth was the other party so insistent that they sign it before walking down the aisle? I know, I know, love is blind. It is sometimes deaf and dumb. Nevertheless, I am astounded at the number of people who seven or eight or 10 or 15 years later will wander into my office and be shocked and offended at the news that what they signed does in fact mean precisely what it says.

I also know that after you are married, when your spouse brings you a quitclaim deed to sign because, "It's just a formality," or, "The bank needs it," you want to believe that is true. I too would want to believe that is true. I might even sign it. I would also know who to blame if it came back to bite me later: myself.

We are now seeing more and more of these agreements. It used to be that they were limited to the rather traditional fact pattern of a previously divorced husband who was marrying wife No. 2 and wanted to preserve his assets. However, frequently both parties have been divorced, and as often as not, Wife No. 2 ("W-2") is a highly paid executive and wants to preserve her assets as well, sometimes with respect to a significantly less financially secure prospective husband. My advice to anyone who is faced with such an agreement is to assume that it is in fact enforceable and means precisely what it says. Read it. It doesn't take someone well versed in legalese to understand that "All right, title and interest to this property together with the rents, profits and dividends, now and in the future shall remain separate," means you don't get any of it, now or later. This is not rocket science.

And, if you are one of the individuals who is presented with such a contract after the marriage or presented with quitclaim deeds or other documents relinquishing title after the marriage and you agree to sign them, you made a choice. I realize that refusing to sign these documents could have caused a terrible family rift, great conflict, trauma, potentially even a divorce. I understand that you may have chosen to sign the document rather than risk any one of those things. Nevertheless, there was a choice and you made it.

In closing, I am reminded of a story told by a colleague. She is a highly experienced family lawyer who was once placed in the position of trying to set aside not only a premarital agreement but two post-marital agreements. Her unfortunate client had not only signed an agreement well in advance of the wedding, but within two or three years thereafter had signed a second and some years thereafter signed a third, all of which not only relinquished any interest in the husband's assets at the time of the marriage, but assets he acquired thereafter, including buildings, businesses, etc. My colleague is a highly effective and articulate attorney and was passionately arguing her client's position before a crusty old judge. At one point during her eloquent argument, the judge stopped her, leaned forward over the bench, looked at her over the top of his half glasses and said, "Counsel, can't your client *read?*"

Take it from me: Lucy VanPelt was wrong.

35

New Mates: The Ghost of Marriage Past

By the time you read this book, some of you will have embarked on a new relationship and will simply be waiting to get the judgment filed in the old one before you can tie the knot with someone new. Or you may in fact be the new mate, reading this book to try to find out what on earth you can do to help your loved one get through it.

There are very specialized problems which will be faced by the new mate.

First and foremost is the temptation to get utterly invested in your new mate's fight. This may be from a need (yours or hers) to prove that you are "there for her." It may be your own sexual jealousy directed toward the person who shared such a major part of her life. Whatever the cause, recognize certain facts:

- You are *not*, repeat *NOT*, objective.

Of course you can't be. You love her. How could you be objective? You are watching someone you love go through terrible pain, probably feeling attacked and perhaps betrayed by someone she trusted for many years. Recognize your feelings and temper your actions accordingly.

- Do not offer legal advice.

Your job is to be lover and supporter. You are not the lawyer, you are not the therapist, and you cannot be either in this case.

Even if you are a lawyer or therapist by profession, you will be unable to function in those roles in a relationship. Take off your lawyer or your therapist hat and put on your lover hat, loving, supportive and nonjudgmental. If you can do all of these things, listen sympathetically, and offer no advice, give yourself a gold star.

If you find yourself getting sucked into the controversy, recognize your lack of objectivity and back off. Don't go with your lover to see the attorney. It's her divorce, not yours, and your mere presence will alter the level and content of communication between your lover and her lawyer. It may also create an automatic waiver of attorney/client privilege, and enable the ex to discover what she and her lawyer discussed.

There is another pitfall into which many new mates stumble. It is extremely difficult to build a new relationship when your lover is preoccupied with the one just ending. Accept certain facts as true: if your lover is going through a divorce, he *is going to be* obsessed with the process. That is a fact of life. The divorce is probably the most traumatic, most significant thing that has happened in your lover's life for many, many years. You will hear about it constantly, and there is going to be endless venting. Frankly, it can be difficult to build a new relationship while the specter of the old one constantly hangs over your dinner table (and your bed). Your lover is not going to be able to give you 100 percent when about 110 percent is being given either to the fight with the ex-spouse, or simply the struggle to stay alive and marginally *compos mentis*. Many characterize divorce as a period of diminished mental capacity, and it frequently is.

Many couples find that the divorce itself becomes a primary factor and glue in their new relationship, i.e., what keeps them together is that they are uniting against a common enemy (W-1). All of the faults and misconduct of W-1 consume their conversation. "The Divorce" is the major event in their lives and in their relationship.

My county has court reporting by videotape. We can leave the trial and have a tape of the entire proceeding which we can pop in our VCRs. This is a wonderful tool to help someone be a more effective witness. It is not entertainment, however. I have been astounded to learn that a client and his new mate have watched a tape of a trial six, seven or eight times! Please . . . it *can't* be that exciting. If it is, the new relationship is in big trouble.

In such situations the couple's primary bond is its alliance against the enemy. When the rival is vanquished (i.e., divorced), the new relationship falls apart, having never built any foundations separate from the process. As new mate, you need to be very careful of this. It is important to be supportive, loving and understanding. It is also important to recognize that if you and your new mate are to have a future, you must build a life together independent of the ghost of marriage past.

36

Mind Games and Button-Pushing

Each of us has an Evil Twin. No matter how lofty our ideals or sincere our motivation as we embark upon the perfect Amicable Divorce, the Evil Twin will try to take over at some point. You know every sore spot, every vulnerable point and every low blow that will get the attention of your spouse. She knows the same about you. Times will come when the temptation to use that information will become almost overwhelming. The operative word here is *almost*. Don't. And if you do, forgive yourself and promise not to do it again. Nothing, but nothing, will cause a divorce to deteriorate from amicable to abysmal in less time than pulling out the heavy artillery. The price is paid in thousands of dollars of attorneys' fees and in sleepless nights anticipating the next court appearance.

I have seen it all too many times. You are getting ready for a four-way settlement meeting with your spouse and both attorneys at one of the attorney's offices. A hearing or a settlement conference is scheduled for a week or two thereafter, and what you really want is to settle it so that you don't have to go to court. You don't want to have to pay your attorney to prepare for the hearing and you certainly don't want to sit across the courtroom from your spouse or suffer the sleepless nights which will precede that "day in court." Equally important, you do not want that court day to be continued for another three or four months because the judge runs out of time.

So you troop into the lawyer's office on the appointed day. Everything goes smoothly until one of you mentions a hot button. It doesn't matter what it is. It could be the suggestion that you were always a Daddy's girl and Daddy will bail you out of this one too, so we don't really need to discuss the issue of who's going to pay for the attorney's fees. It could instead be the implication that he's a lousy parent or she never could take responsibility for her actions. Whatever it is, the result is quite predictable. The situation will escalate until one or the other of the parties is going to storm out of the room and all settlement discussions will end.

If you are the instigator, you may have obtained momentary satisfaction. But what did you really get? Well, you probably got hundreds, if not thousands, of dollars in additional attorneys' fees, another delay, some sleepless nights and very little else.

I promise you that the opportunity to push your spouse's buttons will arise. There is not one of us who is above that image flashing on the mental screen. There is not one of us who is above relishing the delicious sense of visualizing our spouse's response. All I am saying is, do not act on it. You will pay a price. Remember also, that your spouse knows all of your buttons, too.

As a friend of mine is fond of saying, "He who engages in a pissing contest always ends up with wet shoes."

Two other truths to consider:

- The person you are divorcing is not the person you were married to.

- The person you are divorcing is precisely the person you were married to.

No, I haven't lost my mind. Both of those statements are absolutely true. If your spouse was always weak and indecisive or always an arrogant control freak, he is not going to change his stripes simply because you are no longer together. A lousy parent is not likely to turn into a model one. An indifferent mother who would rather play tennis and work out at the gym than attend to the kids is not going to suddenly become Donna Reed. Don't complain to me because your spouse is unreliable and always late for visitation when he was never on time for anything during your ten-year marriage. If you couldn't make him punctual, the judge and I are probably not going to succeed either.

On the other hand, you cannot simply assume that the way your spouse would have responded to a particular situation during the marriage is the way he will during the divorce. For one thing, during the marriage your interests were the same. They are most definitely not the same now. So, even if he always deferred to you in child rearing matters before, he may not now. And if you could always charm him into doing what you wanted, you may find someone else is doing a better job of charming him nowadays . . .

37

Unfinished Business: The Endless Post-Judgment Minuet

By now, you should have realized that I believe divorce should be done by the book, as cleanly and conscientiously as possible. I can assure you that if you don't get it right the first time, you'll be given ample opportunity to try it again, either in the next divorce or more likely, the post-divorce modifications of custody and support.

Here's how it goes. A new client comes into my office. The divorce was final six years ago and the parties still can't speak to each other. They've been involved in a series of bitter conflicts over visitation, support, or the family dog. One of them doesn't pay support on time, and the other withholds visitation. Perhaps the client has had two or three attorneys in the intervening years, each of whom was worse than the one before. Now he wants not only to resolve the current conflict, but to compensate for all the "losses" before.

I decline this case. The parties clearly have unfinished business, and neither is willing to let go of the conflict and get on with life. I don't want to be a part of that dance. I won't be able to solve the problem and he'll never be satisfied.

It is, of course, axiomatic that two people who are committed to fight with one another will find something to fight about,

FEAR AND LOATHING, OR KARMA 101

especially if they have children together. Kids are the worst battle-ground imaginable.

Whether the current conflict is children, money, medical coverage, or an IRS audit of an old tax return, the result is the same. Until you've resolved your unfinished business, the divorce isn't over. It will consume your life for years to come, whether or not you've remarried or moved. As I write this, I think of a new client who appeared in my office today wanting me to represent her on a post-dissolution matter. She cried as she told me how differently she would have handled the initial divorce if she known at the time that it would go on for years. Now, six years later she was still having to respond to his demands for her financial data and he was trying to dictate which school the kid attended. Had she known this at the time of the divorce, she would have approached him very differently then. Well, you're now on notice. It *can* go on for years.

Another manifestation of this dynamic is the couple who keep fighting even though they really have nothing to fight about. On examination, it turns out that to them any relationship, even a hostile one, is better than none. If you find yourself locked in this type of dance, consider what *you* are getting out of it.

This most commonly occurs when there are constant post-divorce battles over visitation, custody and support. Frequently the new mates get drawn into the conflict as well, each feeling the need to protect or stand by his mate, and the situation becomes even more polarized than it was in the beginning.

A couple who is engaged in constant post-divorce fighting has never really divorced. This was brought home to me once by a very wise man. I represented his current wife who, years after the divorce, was still locked in a bitter dispute with her ex-husband. Nothing was too small to trigger a major conflict. Each was remarried, and on one occasion my client brought her new husband into my office for moral support as we discussed the various options available to her in the latest round (Round 27, I think it was). My client's new husband (H-2) listened intently as I described the parameters of the current fight and the options available, as well as what I felt to be reasonable settlement possibilities. My client bristled at the suggestion that she should make any concession whatsoever.

A couple of days later the new husband called me and told me that his conclusion from what he had watched was that his wife, beloved as she was to him, had unfinished business with her ex-husband. He felt that the constant strife was having an adverse impact on their marriage, and until such time as his wife and her ex-husband had resolved their issues, the old marriage would be clouding the new. He wanted to know what I thought about his suggesting that the long-divorced couple go into "post-divorce counseling" together. He felt that both of them would be resistant to it unless it was couched in terms of dealing with issues regarding the children. Before suggesting it, he wanted to know whether I would support the idea. I did, and gave him the names of a couple of outstanding therapists in the area.

The results were better than I had hoped. The new husband (H-2) was able to convince his wife (W-1) that her former husband (H-1) would never straighten out unless a therapist pointed out to him the error of his ways. He told her that H-1 was such an arrogant control freak that no solution imposed upon him by the court would be nearly as successful as one which a therapist could finesse. Meanwhile, he enlisted the support of the new wife (W-2) with the promise that this strategy, at least, had some hope of resolving endless conflict. Frankly, both new mates were sick and tired of the wars of marriage past.

Although it was rocky at the start, it did work. H-1 and W-1 were finally able to disengage, at least enough to stay out of court with one another. H-2 and W-2 got what they wanted, which was to be able to live their own lives without the specter of a former marriage constantly intervening in terms of summonses and court appearances, etc.

I have every reason to believe that the solution was successful in the long term. I am sure they preferred spending their money on vacations rather than legal fees.

If you are engaged in one of these dreadful post-dissolution conflicts, your life will never be your own. Certainly, any new relationship on which you choose to embark will forever be tainted by the specter of the former spouse raising his or her ugly head summoning you back to court. Not only does this create tremendous stress within the family, it is a financial burden as well. I am certain you and your new mate would much rather spend your money on that long-awaited trip to Hawaii rather than on one more visitation modification hearing.

The best way I know to make sure that you avoid this problem is to make sure that you finish your business through the process of the divorce itself. Do it once, and do it right.

Part VI

Solutions

38

Reasonable Solutions to Problems That Come Up In Every Divorce

How to divide the furniture fairly and equitably.

Furnishing a household is an expensive business. It's a rare family that has enough of everything to comfortably supply two. Moreover, at a time when your entire life is disrupted, no one should have to go home to a bare apartment and eat off a card table. It simply isn't right. So here are some very practical suggestions about ways you can solve this problem:

• Inventory the house jointly with your spouse.

Each household consists of a mixture of practical necessities (washer, refrigerator, etc.), sentimental items and valuable pieces (stereo equipment and antiques). For this method, inventory the house with your spouse. (I don't mean that you each have to march from room to room with a clipboard in your hands. One of you should inventory the house and the other should have an opportunity to check the inventory to make sure it is complete and accurate.) Then flip a coin to determine which one of you is going to divide the single list into two lists of approximately equal value. It really doesn't matter who prepares the list. Call one "List A" and the other "List B." Then it's the other party's choice as to which list he wants. This is an excellent method for ensuring that the practical, sentimental and valuable items will be fairly equally sprinkled between the two lists. It avoids the necessity of having to hire appraisers and generally works quite simply. The person making the lists usually "loads" one to be more attractive to the other side. However, he can't afford to load it too much or he'll end up with the short straw. In my experience, once a selection of "A" or "B" is made, there is some horse-trading back and forth and everyone goes away relatively satisfied that it was fair.

- If you can afford it, duplicate the necessities *at community expense*.

Purchase another refrigerator, another washer/dryer, another set of dishes, towels, etc. You then trade off; one of you gets the new toaster, one of you gets the old one. You reverse it for the blenders. This way, each party has the dignity of a fully furnished household (or relatively so) and you avoid the nasty tug of war that frequently ensues in furniture divisions. This method is a must for the division of records and CDs that you both love, favorite books, etc.

- For God's sake, the kids' furniture goes with the kids.

It is not valued or divided. In fact, it is my belief that for the sake of the children, the community should purchase kids' furniture for use at the visiting parent's home. This is not done as a favor to your ex-spouse. It is done to ensure that your children have a safe, comfortable and nurturing *home* at both residences. Children should not to have to sleep on cots when visiting their parents. Divorce is stressful enough for them without uncomfortable and unsafe physical surroundings.

Pets

Pets should go with the party to whom they are emotionally connected, regardless of whether the puppy or kitten was originally a gift to the other party.

Family Photos and Videos

These should be divided equally between the parties without fail. If you can afford it, duplicate the special ones at community expense so you each have a copy. Ditto address books.

Financial Records and Tax Returns

I've described the importance of sharing financial data in other chapters. Each of you should have a complete set of tax returns and the important financial files such as the purchases and sales of real properties. You may need them for future tax audits, for rolling over capital gain in a new residence, and your attorney will certainly need them. Don't require a formal request to the Internal Revenue Service. Instead, copy them at the beginning.

Canceling Credit Cards

The average American family is going to have several credit cards, most of them with outstanding balances that they cannot afford to pay in full at the moment of separation. Make sure that you and your spouse each have complete knowledge of balances on all of your existing credit cards. Also, make sure that you know if there are old open credit accounts which you may have paid off but never closed.

A good way to accomplish this is to request your own credit report. Although not a perfect solution, this will give you a place to start identifying not only the extent of your debt, but the existence of any old credit cards or credit lines. Most of us have old credit accounts which we have not used in years and about which we have usually forgotten. These need to be canceled. Don't wait until you find out that your ex has borrowed $20,000 on an old credit line that you forgot you had signed on ten years ago. You may still be liable to the bank even if the divorce court ultimately orders your spouse to pay the debt.

You and your spouse should each have complete information as to the existing credit cards, debt, and any open cards or lines which may still be in existence. I am not an advocate of canceling credit without notice. Assuming that you and your spouse are still communicating, you should discuss it and determine which one of you is going to use which card(s), who is going to make the minimum payments on which obligations and how are you going to account for those payments between the two of you. Any open credit cards with zero balances or any outstanding credit lines should be jointly closed.

This way, nobody has any nasty surprises when they try to use a credit card and find it rejected, nor does either party have the ability to borrow against an unknown credit line without notice.

Childrens' Unreimbursed Medical Expenses

One of the more common post-dissolution tugs of war involves the handling of medical, dental and orthodontia insurance, expenses and reimbursements for the kids. Typically, there is an order requiring either or both parents to cover the children on insurance available through employment. One parent takes the kid to the doctor (and advances the cost), and the other has to process the claim (and perhaps pockets the reimbursement check). Sometimes this is done with the intent of playing games, sometimes it is just out of reluctance to deal directly with the ex to resolve the accounting.

Instead, I suggest opening a separate bank account jointly, for the sole purpose of covering these expenses. Each parent deposits an agreed amount at the beginning, and each is authorized to sign checks. There should be an order, or at least a written agreement detailing the rules. All agreed expenses are paid from the account, including that initial visit to the doctor. All insurance reimbursement checks are redeposited into the account. Each party has access to the statements, and when the balance drops below a designated amount, each party replenishes it. Here are some suggested terms:

- Each parent deposits $500 (or some other agreed amount) when the account is opened.

Sometimes the contributions are apportioned according to the timeshare, that is, if Mom has the kids 60% and Dad has 40%, the deposits are done 60/40. Alternatively, the deposits are 50/50 or are apportioned according to the parties' respective incomes after adjusting for support.

- The parent who is most likely to take the kids to the doctor has primary control of the checkbook, subject to accounting.

- Agree on what expenses will be covered.

Sometimes there is a dollar limit, i.e., advance approval is required for non-emergency treatment of over $300. Sometimes orthodontia is treated separately. The payments can be limited to routine medical and dental care. However, with all the activities kids are involved in these days, the list can be readily expanded. For example, if you don't want to get into a battle over whether the child support is supposed to cover soccer camp or music lessons, you might want to include some of the following:

Music, tennis, dance and other lessons
Sports camps
Tutors
School fees
Ski or other sporting equipment
Yearbook and other non-recurring fees
Other "extras" you both agree on

- Decide on the timing and method of replenishment.

I have found this to work well if the parents stick to the rules. Certainly the kids love it because they don't miss the soccer camp registration deadline because Mom and Dad are jockeying for position about who should advance the fee and take the risk of not being reimbursed.

Wills and Estate Planning

If you are contemplating divorce, you may not want your soon-to-be-ex spouse to be the heir to your estate. You and your spouse probably signed reciprocal wills at some time in the past and you should review these to see if you want to make a change. I have had some clients who chose to name their spouses heirs after the divorce. Most don't, and wish to change their wills to make their children or other family members their heirs.

At the early stage of the divorce, you won't know what property you are going to have in the ultimate division. Therefore, it is impossible for you to do a comprehensive estate plan. However, you can do an interim will and revoke the prior will. Then, when the property division is completed, you can make an estate plan which is appropriate to your financial situation.

39

Taking Responsibility for Your Own Lawyer's Conduct

What happens when you are part way through the divorce and find you are not comfortable with the strategies or approaches of your attorney?

We've already talked about how to select a lawyer, and hopefully you've made a wise choice. However, there are times when you find it simply is not going the way you thought it would.

The first rule is that it is *your* divorce. You will be living with the consequences of the strategies adopted and the decisions that you and your attorney make for the rest of your natural life. Your attorney will not. Therefore, the ultimate decision-making authority and the ultimate responsibility are yours.

We've already assumed that you want the divorce to be as smooth and amicable as possible and that you are going to insist on good communication with your attorney. If you find that the conduct of your case is making you uncomfortable, discuss it with your attorney. If you are still uncomfortable, change attorneys. It is your responsibility to tell your attorney if you believe her conduct is too belligerent, if you believe that unnecessary discovery is being done or you want a different strategy adopted. Your attorney may want your instructions in writing. That is perfectly fair. Recognize that you are not a lawyer and are not objective. If after seriously considering your goals, the strategy adopted so far, and your attorney's recommendations, you still believe a different strategy is required, you should not hesitate to give those instructions in writing to your attorney. If they are not followed, make a change.

I have already said that selecting your attorney is probably the single most important determining factor in charting the course of your divorce. Even among equally competent attorneys, there will be wide variations in style, tactics and strategy. After getting into the case, you may find that the style you originally thought was going to work best is counterproductive or is one with which you are simply not comfortable.

I am not talking about firing your lawyer the first time you disagree on a strategy. I am talking about taking responsibility.

I have always been of the theory that anyone can make one mistake in the selection of an attorney. I have never hesitated to give a second opinion to a client and will generally agree to substitute in as the second attorney in a case if I think I can help. However, I won't agree to be attorney number three, four or five. When a prospective client comes in with a litany of complaints about the four or five attorneys who have previously represented him, each one worse than the last, my antennae go up. If someone has been through that many attorneys, it tells me that either he is the worst judge of character in recorded history or he is more interested in finding someone who will tell him what he wants to hear than in hearing the truth. He will continue to look for someone else to blame rather than take responsibility for his own role in the divorce.

So, if you've started the divorce and you're feeling uncomfortable about the way the case is being handled, get a second opinion or even a third. If, after doing so, you are still unhappy with the course your attorney has adopted, that is the time to make a change, and the sooner the better. Don't wait until a counterproductive strategy has been put in place and then go to a new attorney to try to undo all the harm that has been done while you've been trying to figure out what to do. Make the decision and act on it.

The corollary is, be sure your next choice is an improvement. The more times you've changed attorneys, the fewer really competent attorneys will be willing to talk to you, much less take over the case.

40

Keeping a Rein On
Fees and Costs

"Yes, Virginia, you will have to pay for it."

One of the most important things that you can do to retain a realistic attitude toward your divorce from the beginning is to assume that you are in fact going to have to pay your own attorney's fees. I have had this conversation with literally hundreds of clients. The old days where the husband paid all the fees because he was the traditional sole wage earner are long gone in most jurisdictions. Many courts have now adopted the philosophy that the fees on *both* sides should be paid from the marital estate. The theory, of course, is that it took two of you to make the marriage and it takes two to make the divorce. Although this sometimes favors the side which unreasonably runs up the fees, in general I find the philosophy a sound one.

Do yourself a favor: Realize at the beginning that you are likely to pay all of your own fees and, more important, you will likely pay them with after-tax dollars. This means that in this day of higher tax brackets, in order to pay $1,000 worth of attorneys' fees in your divorce, you will have to earn $1,500 to $1,800. Unless you happen to be sitting on a pot of gold, it's going to hurt.

Before the fees run into the tens of thousands and you suddenly realize that there is insufficient money to pay them, become involved. You are not powerless. Here are some things which you can do from the outset to help you keep fees and costs under control:

- Provide every bit of information and financial data that you can to your attorney without the necessity of subpoenas.

Subpoenas are costly and time-consuming. If you have family financial records in the file cabinet at home, take a weekend and go through them. Take the documents to your attorney. If your spouse wants a set of the documents, make a copy available at his expense. This means that neither side will be required to send out subpoenas for documents that are readily available. I cannot begin to tell you how many times I have received a subpoena from opposing counsel for records which were available from his own client or in the file cabinet at the house.

- Give your attorney financial information that is as complete as possible, even if it isn't perfect.

If you haven't historically been active in managing the family finances and have a secretive spouse, you may in fact not have access to much information. However, if you know that there is (or at least was) an account at ABC Bank, even if you don't know which branch or the account number, tell your attorney. This at least gives him a lead on where to go looking for the money. It is financially prohibitive to subpoena all of the possible asset repositories where your spouse may have stashed the cash. Private investigation services are expensive and the results are spotty at best. Anything you can do to narrow the field will help keep your fees and costs to a manageable level.

- If you don't have records but know where to get them, do so.

For example, banks frequently charge a great deal for subpoenas of their records, particularly if they are voluminous. However, if you, as a signatory on the account, go to the bank to get the records, the charge may well be significantly less. Additionally, if you know that there are specific checks you need, you don't need to get all of them. Get the checks that you know you need. You can always go back and get others later if they are needed.

- If your attorney doesn't ask you what financial records you have or have access to, ask *him* what you can do to help prepare your case.

Get a list of the information your attorney is going to want and start doing your own leg work. This doesn't mean that you should be practicing law or earning a degree as a paralegal. However, you probably have a greater ability to get information informally than your attorney does. Anything that you can do to accomplish this will mean one less subpoena or deposition.

- When your attorney receives records from the other side, go through them yourself.

This is very important. Your attorney cannot know everything about you or your life. There may be a notation in a check register which would mean absolutely nothing to your attorney or her paralegal. However you know that it is your spouse's best buddy from college with whom he always had financial deals going on the side. Only you will know that the appearance of this name in your spouse's financial transactions is a red flag to possible diversion of funds. Your attorney will have no way of knowing this unless you become involved in the process yourself.

- At every stage in the proceeding, do a cost/benefit analysis.

For many of you, this will be the first time you have had to do such a formal analysis. It's time to learn how. Suppose that your spouse has filed a document with the court which contains a lie, a boldfaced, absolutely provable lie. However, if the lie is about a $600 item and it is going to cost you $500 to subpoena the records necessary to prove the lie, or double that to take the deposition, what is the point? Discuss your discovery plan with your attorney. Find out what subpoenas she thinks are important and what depositions should be taken. Find out the approximate cost of each of these and the approximate benefit *in financial* terms if the discovery turns up the evidence you expect. Consider also the likely risk of discovery not being fruitful.

If you happen to live in one of those jurisdictions where the courts charge these fees to the person who is caught in the lie, so be it. However, don't count on it. Attorneys' fees are almost always the last issue settled, and even a relatively good claim for fees frequently gets swept under the rug as part of an overall resolution.

Accordingly, at each stage of discovery, you should know the likely benefits of the discovery and the attendant cost.

Sometimes your attorney will want to send out a subpoena which you do not think is worth the cost. I have set forth in much greater detail in the previous chapter ("Taking Responsibility for Your Own Lawyer's Conduct") my theories about who is ultimately responsible for the conduct of the case. It is *your* case. If you really believe, despite your attorney's advice, that the proposed discovery is not justified, instruct your attorney not to pursue it. If she asks you to put those instructions in writing to protect her from a later malpractice claim, comply. It isn't fair for you to tell your attorney not to take steps to protect you and then, when the result turns out to be something other than you had hoped, to use the fact that there is no written record to sue her. If you are going to take responsibility, take it. If, on the other hand, you don't want to take the responsibility, you will pay for it. Remember, your attorney's ethical duty is to perform what is called "due diligence" to protect you. He can't afford to guess or gamble with your future. You, however, can take calculated risks, but only if you involve yourself in the process. Interestingly, more attorneys get sued by former clients for not doing enough discovery than for doing too much. Go figure.

Don't passively stand on the sidelines as the fees creep up to $10,000 and $20,000 and then suddenly decide that it wasn't worth it and you can't afford to pay for it. Too many people then settle out of panic instead of taking a reasoned approach from the beginning.

• Don't use your lawyer as a therapist.

One of the prime causes for fees which go literally through the roof is that you are constantly in your lawyer's office for moral support. This is a lousy use of your lawyer's time and your money. You can probably hire a first-rate therapist for a lower hourly rate than you are paying your attorney. This goes for the attorney's staff as well. They are genuinely interested in helping people, or they wouldn't have chosen to work in such an emotionally demanding career. That doesn't mean they are qualified or wish to serve as your shrink.

- If you are pursuing a fight to score emotional points against your spouse, I guarantee you that your legal fees will be out of proportion to the satisfaction ultimately attained.

If you insist on litigating the minutia just to prove that your spouse has lied in court documents, or prove to the judge what a scum your ex may be, you will incur a fee bill all out of proportion to the value received. Your spouse may be a walking oil slick. Chances are that the judge has figured that out for himself. If you insist on paying your lawyer to marshal all of the "evidence" of the lies that he told you for the last 20 years, you will be faced with a fee bill you will not want to pay. Rather than get into a fight over fees with your lawyer, why not be realistic about it from the beginning? And don't wait until the legal fees equal the equity in your house before taking control.

41

Goals:
Part II

By now you have had some opportunity to think about what is important to you.

Recognizing that at the end of the process you are only going to have about half of what you thought you owned at the beginning (since as couples we all think we own all of it collectively), you should have spent some time thinking about which half you would prefer.

I have already cautioned you not to make too many irrevocable decisions in the early months because your goals will change as you get more perspective on the separation. But assuming you have already come through that part of the process, you should be in a position to make some decisions. Since you are not going to get it all, what would you really like to have?

For many of you, goal setting will be second nature. Either you do it daily in your business or it is simply a knack which you have. For others, it will be a struggle to simply learn the mechanics of how to make a decision and set priorities. It may be as simple as taking a sheet of paper and writing down the pros and cons in parallel columns. Some of you may let options roll around in the back of your heads until the correct one pops out, as if by magic. Others will be able to weigh the probable consequences of your decision at lightning speed. Whatever method works will be the right method for you. Here are some suggestions of things you might consider.

One of the issues which causes the most angst is whether to keep or sell the house. For some of you this will not be a decision at all; it will be a financial necessity because neither of you can afford to keep it. For others, it will consume months of agony.

Suppose the mortgage is $200 per month because you and your spouse have been there since dirt was invented. However, you may be thinking, "The house is too big for me," or "It's too much upkeep," etc. It may be a financial disaster to sell the house. You may be motivated by emotional considerations ("There are too many memories there"). I have asked many a client to consider whether is it better to live in a house with a $200 per month mortgage payment and lots of memories or a condo on which your payment is $1,400 and you live on spaghetti for the rest of your natural life? This is a *financial* decision. Keep in mind you will be assuming potential future capital gains tax. Now, you may make the decision for emotional reasons, i.e., you may determine that it is worth the additional $1,200 a month to you not to be surrounded by familial memories. It is clearly your right and your decision. However, recognize that you are making an emotional decision rather than a financial one and be certain that you are willing to live with the consequences before the "for sale" sign goes up.

If the house really is too big for you, this may be the time to sell it and share the capital gain with your spouse. All these factors need to be included in your decision. This is where your attorney, accountant or financial planner can be of great assistance.

Perhaps you are in the reverse situation. You assume that you "have to" keep the house because you've got the kids. Many kids are quite adaptable and yours may be among them. Make the decision based upon the facts as they exist in *your* case. Be willing to consider other options and don't assume that just because it has always been this way, it has to be in the future. And if the house is a drafty old money pit, you and the kids could have a wonderful time shopping for your new home together.

I have had clients tell me that they simply can't stand to spend one more month in the family homestead because of all of the baggage and memories that it carries; others believed they would utterly fall apart if required to leave their sanctuaries. Only you know what is most important to you. The important thing is that you understand the emotional and financial price of either course of action, quantify both and make the best decision you can under the circumstances.

Once you have made the decision, LET IT GO. We could all spend the rest of our lives second guessing ourselves with what-ifs. Make a deal with yourself that if you have made the best decision you can under the facts and circumstances then known to you, you will not beat yourself about the head and shoulders about it for years to come. Decide and move on.

42

How to Evaluate
a Settlement Offer

Sooner or later, you are going to be called upon to either make or respond to a settlement proposal, perhaps several during the course of your divorce. If you are not accustomed to negotiation, it is going to be important to educate yourself so that you don't lose an opportunity to resolve the case satisfactorily outside of court.

It is my belief that court is a last resort. The only reason you and your soon-to-be ex would be sitting across a courtroom from one another is because one or both sides have failed to realistically assess their case and negotiate a reasonable settlement.

Sometimes a total settlement simply cannot be pulled off and part of the case must be tried. However, I have rarely seen a case between two sane people in which at least some of the issues cannot be agreed. Perhaps you are at a complete impasse on the value of the family business but at least can agree on where your kids should live. Perhaps you can agree who is going to be in the house and the value of the house, but can't seem to get over the issue of support. At least agree on the things you can. This will mean that the judge will have more time to devote to those areas where you really are stuck. It also assures that, at least as to the issues you've settled, you (and not the judge) will be deciding where you make concessions.

The toughest situations are where you both want the same thing. You are both invested in having the house and no other house will do. However, if you find yourself in that position and are about to walk into a court room to have the judge decide, at least make sure that you have made every effort to resolve the case on reasonable terms.

Before describing what to do in this situation, I'd like to spend a little time on what not to do.

Many clients have assured me throughout the course of a bitter, hard-fought divorce that all they want is to settle. I have learned that phrase can mean very different things to different people. If the "settlement offer" invariably comes down to the sum total of your best case on every issue, this is *not* negotiating. It is nothing more than insisting on having everything your way. Unless your spouse and his attorney are both idiots, you are wasting your time and money.

You will be equally unsuccessful at settling your case if you define every concession as a loss. Divorce, as with marriage and life itself, is a series of compromises and if you start out with the mindset that the other side "wins" every time you concede a point, there will be precious few concessions and no real chance for settlement.

So what *should* you do?

Know your best-case and worst-case positions. Thoroughly and objectively analyze your case with your attorney and understand precisely what the most likely winners and losers are. Ask your attorney, issue by issue, what she thinks the judge will do. She will be unlikely to give you a firm commitment in all areas because so many of these areas are within the discretion of the judge. However, she should be able to tell you within some reasonable percentage. This exercise is very helpful for both of you, as it forces you to step back and quite critically and dispassionately look at the weaknesses of your case. One of the first hallmarks of a good attorney is that she knows the weaknesses of her own case, knows how to try to parlay them into a good settlement, and when to cut to the chase and concede a loser.

In evaluating your best and worst case scenarios, you must assume that neither you nor your ex is going to get everything you want. Family law judges loathe sending people out of their courtrooms empty-handed. Therefore, chances are very good that even if the judge has to stretch a little bit, she's going to find a way to make sure that everyone goes away with something. This means that for starters, you'd better be willing to decide before you go into court which issues you would rather concede if you have to.

Analyze the other side's case using the same process. You may figure wrong, but after all, the opposing party is the person you know best in the world. If you think he is utterly committed to ending up with the house and in your secret heart of hearts something else is more important to you, file that information away. I smell a settlement somewhere. Is there some way you can trade things you don't really want (but the other side does) for things you do want? The corollary of this is, of course, that even if you don't particularly want it right now, don't give it away until you're sure you can't trade it for something you do want.

Package your proposal in such a way that the other side wins something, too. Preferably, package it in such a way that it looks like the other side is winning a whole lot more than he is. Don't get silly about this, but after all, the goal is to have him accept it. If there's nothing in it for him and he has nothing to lose by going to trial, why on God's earth shouldn't he roll the dice?

Strategize the settlement negotiations with your attorney. Find out your attorney's style of negotiating and what strategy she thinks would be most likely to work, given the facts of your case and the personalities of your spouse and the other attorney.

In my negotiations, I frequently oppose attorneys with whom I have had other cases and other settlement negotiations. I have formed an opinion of their styles (and, quite frankly they have formed one of mine).

At this stage in the proceedings, I always hope there's a competent attorney on the other side. Two skilled attorneys will each know an approximate range within which the case should resolve, given all of the facts, the law, the risks and the judge's personality, as well as the personalities of the litigants. We're not always right, but more often than not, there's a range. I know I'm going to get to that range sooner or later and so does the other attorney, if he has any idea what he's doing. It is a waste of my time and my client's money to make a settlement proposal that is way outside the range. Accordingly, when I commence negotiations with a new attorney, I always make a point of telling him that my offer is designed to be a very serious, mid-ground compromise and is not simply an invitation to negotiate. Therefore, I will thoroughly and carefully evaluate the risks of my case before the first settlement offer is made, and then I will probably not move a great deal, certainly not outside the range I've already established for myself. This means we get to the bottom line much faster with much less money spent in attorney fees, and I think everyone ends up happier in the long run.

This is an area in which I tend not to play "hide-the-ball." When I'm making a first-time settlement proposal to an attorney I've never negotiated with before, I'm quite likely to define my expectations about negotiation right in the letter. This shortcuts a great deal of expensive back and forth. I don't respect attorneys who make either a ridiculously high or ridiculously low offer. "Here's my proposal: I get everything and you get nothing. Offer expires at 5:00 p.m. tomorrow." These tactics may work in other areas of the law, but I find them counterproductive where family law is concerned. They may well draw a sanction in some courts.

The worst thing about having an incompetent attorney on the other side is that although you might assume she would give away the store because she doesn't know what she's doing, the opposite is actually true. Because she doesn't know how to evaluate the risks of her own case, she tends to dig in and refuse to concede even the obvious losers. (See Chapter 8, "Why You Want the Your Spouse to Have a Good Lawyer, Too"). This runs up legal fees and requires unnecessary trials. It may be easy to beat up on the stupid attorney at trial, but I always find it quite frustrating and so do the litigants. It isn't fair to the client who's being well represented because he is having to go through a trial he neither needs nor wants simply to get to a reasonable solution. It is equally unfair for the client who is being badly represented because he is being given a false sense of security that he is going to win every issue and, of course, it isn't true.

Always, always, always factor the cost of fighting a particular issue into any evaluation of a settlement proposal. If you've done as I suggested, you already have a relatively clear understanding of your best and worst case scenarios. You should not only be advised where the range of settlement might be, but on which issues you are weak. Add to this entire soup the cost of trial. By that I do not mean just the attorney and accountant or other expert witness fees. These can be substantial and run to the tens of thousands of dollars even for a relatively short trial. There is also the cost of being prepared for trial and then finding that the court's calendar is too busy and there is no court available. This means that you come back two or three months later. You'd think that you wouldn't have to prepare for trial all over again because, of course, all the work was done . . . right? I'm afraid not. Property values and bank balances may have changed, requiring updates. Trial notes have gotten cold and you are going to pay your attorney to prepare again so that he is on top of all of the evidence, the witnesses and the testimony. When trials are continued more than once, the costs become horrendous.

Finally, consider the emotional wear and tear that you, your spouse and your children will suffer if you go to trial.

I don't mean that you should roll over and play dead at the thought of going to trial, but you should quantify the cost. Educate yourself about the risks and benefits and recognize that nothing is utterly predictable. Let me give you two examples.

- You say to your attorney, "I realize he's insisting on a value of the house that's thousands of dollars higher than the market. However, this has been dragging on for two years and I simply can't stand it anymore. I'll do *anything* to get this over with. Just accept the offer and be done with it."

Six months or a year from now when you're comfortably ensconced in your house, the emotional pressure that caused you to simply throw up your hands and give in is a remote memory. You are going to start thinking of all the uses you might have had for that $30,000 (or $10,000 or $5,000), and human nature being what it is, you will probably conclude it wasn't worth it.

- Or, you say to your attorney, "You and I both know that they're being outrageous in insisting on such a high value for my business. Not only is our appraisal lower, even their appraisal is lower. This is just extortion."

You may be right; it is. I hate giving in to extortion as much as the next guy, except that sometimes it is cost-effective. If the other side is insisting on an unreasonable position but the cost to you of giving in is less than the cost of actually trying the case, you may want to seriously consider compromising that issue. This is particularly true if there's a chance that you will have to pay the other side's fees as well. I know, this isn't fair. But who said anything about fairness?

Vindication carries a price tag. I realize that many states now allow an order for attorney's fees in the form of sanctions, so that the unreasonable party (or an attorney, for that matter) can be ordered to pay your attorney's fees for fighting stupid issues. These orders can be extremely difficult to obtain and are used only reluctantly by most judges. Accordingly, in evaluating a proposal, assume that you're going to be paying your own fees and factor that cost into your analysis.

Quantify, quantify, quantify. When evaluating an offer, you have to be able to estimate with some degree of confidence the probable cost of going to court versus the probable cost of conceding whatever issue you're being asked to yield. Only you can quantify the emotional cost. Your attorney can help you with the financial part. However, this is another place to remember that no matter how predictable we think a particular fact pattern will be with a particular judge, anything can, and does, happen in trial.

Sooner or later, almost everyone comes to an issue about which they say, "It's not the money. It's the principle of the thing." Those words inevitably make me cringe. My reply is always to insist that the client quantify the principle. I ask her, "Is this principle worth $300 to you? $3,000? $30,000?" At some point on this continuum, you are going to find an amount you are not willing to pay for the principle. Once you have done that, take one more hard look at yourself to determine whether you really are willing to pay the price just to be proven "right." Then take out your checkbook and write the check.

This is a prime area for "sellers' remorse." Just as the party who concedes too much to just get it over finds six months later that it probably wasn't worth it, the individual who insists on fighting "for the principle" invariably reaches the same conclusion. Once you've been proven "right" and wrapped yourself in the American flag, couldn't you think of a better use for that $5,000? I could. A trip to Europe or maybe even your kids' braces comes to mind. Think about it.

Remember, whatever the ultimate settlement, you're probably going to be unhappy with it. This is simple human nature. Before you and your spouse split, you jointly owned everything. Now you find you own only half of it, and "it" may have been substantially depleted by the cost of litigation and supporting two households. Anyone who's ever negotiated a business deal knows there is give and take. There are things you wish you could have kept that you had to give up, and in exchange you got something else. People who are not familiar with negotiation frequently find this the most baffling part of the entire process. Their usual reaction is to simply dig in their heels and refuse to settle for fear of making the "wrong" decision. These are the cases that go to trial and shouldn't.

So if you find yourself contemplating a divorce and you're not comfortable negotiating business transactions, educate yourself.

There are many good books out there on negotiation skills and techniques. Buy them, read them and, most important, to the extent that it is possible, take as objective and rational a view of your own divorce as you can. I always tell clients to pretend it's a business deal. We know it isn't, but if we can pretend so at least for purposes of the negotiation process, we will do a lot better.

And if you are the hot shot negotiator of the western world, recognize that you are personally invested in this particular negotiation, and your lack of objectivity will make you much less effective than when you negotiate a business deal.

There is no "perfect" solution. Make the best decision you can under the circumstances and move on.

43

Disengaging

"Evil will simply disappear when given nothing to push against."
Tao te Ching

It takes two to make a war. It also takes two to settle. This may sound like a *non sequitur* but it really isn't. Even if you are divorcing the asshole of the western world, you *can* disengage to some extent. You won't be able to do it, however, unless and until you understand that the conflict of the divorce had its roots in the conflict of the marriage. That's another way of saying that you both have responsibility for the negativity of the process.

This is not a book about psychology. It is a book about the process of divorce. However, there is a huge amount of psychology which goes into a simple, common-sense approach.

If you are involved in a war that you don't want, take a hard look at what you are doing to further the conflict and, more important, what you can do to disengage. There are ways to disengage without sacrificing important legal and financial goals. You will never achieve it, however, if you are still trying to:

- Get even for past treatment.

- Catch up or recoup what you gave away in the past which you now perceive as overly generous.

- Engage in any kind of payback or one-upmanship.

- Prove that you are "right."

- Prove that it's your spouse's fault.

- Prove that your spouse is a bad parent.

- All of the above and more.

These are all issues which you should examine with the assistance of your therapist. If you can't afford a therapist, take a good hard look at yourself in the mirror.

I have found that it is simply impossible to look yourself in the eye in the mirror and lie. If you are at this stage and having to figure it out for yourself, pull a chair up in front of the mirror. It might be helpful to have a box of Kleenex handy as well. Choose a time when you know you will be uninterrupted for at least half an hour. Promise yourself that you will be absolutely honest.

When you have done all of the above, ask yourself the hard questions. What are *you* still getting out of the fight? What are *you* doing to promote it? In what ways are *you* engaging in the conflict? Ask all of these questions while holding a fixed gaze into your own eyes in the mirror. If you find that you look away when you try to answer any of these questions, you are lying to yourself. As soon as you find you can't look yourself in the eye in the mirror and answer your question, you have hit pay dirt. That's the issue you need to work on. Until you have resolved it, you will remain engaged in the conflict yourself and you will not be able to move beyond it.

If you want to end the war, you have to let go. You will never be out of the war until you let go of the relationship. Even if you are giving away the store out of martyrdom or guilt, you are continuing the conflict albeit in a passive/aggressive way.

I have seen divorce wars go on for years after the final judgment. People who are truly committed to war can fight about everything from how the kids' hair is cut to who takes Jason to baseball practice or anything else that requires them to interact. I remember talking to a client whose divorce had deteriorated into monumental conflicts over minute post-judgment issues. The other party was, if anything, more bitter and vindictive than the day the marriage ended. As my client was expressing her frustration at the waste of time, money and energy being spent on minutia, I suggested that she simply disengage. She looked at me in horror. "But then *he'd* win!" Yes, this time he would win and maybe the next time and maybe the next time. Really . . . the issues at stake were whether the visit ended at 6:30 or 7:30, and the like. They were hardly life-threatening. I thought there was a reasonably good chance that after a while, things would calm down when the ex found there was nothing to push against. One always can (and should) hold firm on an important issue which involves children's welfare and the like. However, it takes two to fight about how Johnny's hair is cut.

If you want a graphic illustration of what negativity can do to a couple, I strongly suggest that you see the movie *War of The Roses* which was released a few years ago. I found it to be a brilliant (and quite accurate) demonstration of what can happen when two people allow conflict to consume them.

Interestingly, the movie didn't do particularly well at the box office. I couldn't understand it until I saw it in the movie theater and realized I was the only one laughing. Of course, I had seen every one of the stunts these people pulled on one another, so it was old hat to me. I was able to appreciate the satire while recognizing the reality.

Leaving the movie theater, many of the couples were not making eye contact with one another. The movie cut too close to the bone. That's precisely what made the satire so delicious but disturbing. Several couples were obviously uncomfortable. The next morning I called opposing counsel on a particularly nasty divorce and offered to make a deal with her. I told her I would make my client go see the movie if she would do the same with hers. Ultimately, both of our clients were so invested in the conflict that I don't believe either of them ever saw the movie. Certainly neither of them stopped living it and creating new variations.

If you are seriously wrestling with this issue, be honest with yourself. Sit down and make a list of what is important to you in life. Revise the list periodically and choose your con-flicts accordingly.

If all other motivations fail, imagine this one. Your spouse wants to fight for the next 20 years over everything from what time the sun will rise to what day of the week it is. If you simply disengage and get on with your own life, it will drive him nuts.

44

More
Resources

The good news is that there are an increasing number of excellent resources to help you get through the divorce process. Some are better than others, and I encourage you to keep looking for the ones which speak to you. Among my favorites are the following:

How to Survive the Loss of a Love by Melba Colgrove, Harold H. Bloomfield and Peter McWilliams (1991) Prelude Press

This little gem of a book was originally published in 5,000 copies. It struck a nerve and has more than 2,500,000 in print. It is the best resource I know to help people surviving a loss (in fact, any kind of a loss). I cannot recommend it highly enough. It is widely available.

Crazy Time: Surviving Divorce and Building a New Life by Abigail Trafford (1992) Harper

I first heard about this one from my clients, with whom it is a favorite. The psychology is excellent. It is a good guide to help the healing start.

My Kids Don't Live With Me Anymore by Doreen Virtue (1988) Comp-Care Publishers

The author focuses on the custody process. She offers excellent insight into the emotional issues involved, and the book is filled with practical suggestions for coping. This is the best I've been able to find of its kind.

The Divorce Book by Matthew McKay, Ph.D., Peter D. Roger, Ph.D., Joan Blades, J.D. and Richard Gosse (1984) New Harbinger Publications

Don't let the date throw you off. This is a very thoughtful work. Chapter 12, "Telling the Children" is an excellent resource.

Getting Divorced Without Ruining Your Life by Sam Margulies, J.D., Ph.D. (1992) Simon & Schuster

This is a very practical guide to the emotional and financial aspects of the process. The legal information is more specific to the East Coast, but quite sensible and helpful for anyone seeking practical knowledge about the process.

Life After Divorce by Sharon Wegscheider-Cruse, (1994) Health Communications, Inc.

I particularly recommend the Legal Guidelines contained in Chapter 4 and Chapter 8 on Helping Children Cope with Divorce.

Divorce and New Beginnings: An Authoritative Guide to Recovery and Growth, Solo Parenting and Stepfamilies by Genevieve Clapp, Ph.D. (1992) John Wiley & Sons, Inc.

There is an excellent section on divorce from the child's perspective. It is a good resource for information on single parenting and blended families.

Second Chances by Judith S. Wallerstein and Sandra Blakeslee (1989) Houghton Mifflin Company

Judy Wallerstein was one of the pioneers in studying the actual effects of divorce on children using a longitudinal study (together with Joan B. Kelly). *Second Chances* is the follow up work which is highly acclaimed by therapists and attorneys alike and is a landmark in the field. See also the original book, *Surviving the Breakup: How Children and Parents Cope With Divorce*, Wallerstein and Kelly, (1980) Basic Books.

Divorce Hangover by Anne M. Walther, M.S. (1991) Pocket Books (Simon & Schuster).

I found this a very practical guide to ending the "Endless Post-Judgment Minuet" referred to in Chapter 37.

Between Love & Hate: A Guide to Civilized Divorce by L. Gold (1992) Plenum Press

This is one of the best and most balanced. It offers excellent insight into the psychology of divorce and realistic use of the legal process. Highly recommended.

Mom's House, Dad's House: Making Shared Custody Work by I. Ricci. (1980) Colier Books/ Macmillan

This set the standard for joint custody books for many years and is still quite helpful.

The Good Divorce by Constance Ahrens (1994) HarperCollins

Connie Ahrens' book is a helpful look at modern families of divorce. It straddles the cusp between the popular market and a scholarly research work. Particularly useful is her use of neutral terms and practical approach.

Books for Children

Dinosaurs Divorce, a Guide for Changing Families by L. & M. Brown (1986) Joy Street Books/ Little, Brown

Two Homes to Live In, a Child's-Eye View of Divorce, by B. Hazen (1983) Human Sciences Press/Plenum

This one is best for kids under 6.

Articles

If you really want to know about the psychological effects of divorce on children, go the source material. There are countless scholarly articles and studies out now. The Center for the Family in Transition in Marin County, California has an extensive reprint list of articles on the subject. The list can be ordered from them by writing the Center at 5725 Paradise Drive, Building G, Suite 300, Corte Madera, CA 94925. I frequently give a copy of the list to clients and suggest they order reprints of the studies and articles which seem most relevant to their own kids' ages and situations.

Video and Audio

There is a wonderful video called *Listen to the Children: Divorce Education for Parents*. It was done by the Family Law Section of the State Bar of Michigan. It is produced and distributed by Victor/Harder Productions, Inc. (313) 661-6730. Many other bar associations have also produced videos for parents.

John Bradshaw does an audiotape *On Surviving Divorce; an Emotional Survival Kit* (1989) which is available from Bradshaw Cassettes, P.O. Box 720947, Houston, TX 77272. He even has an 800 number: 1-800-6-BRADSHAW.

Support Groups

In addition to traditional support groups run by therapists and churches, there are countless other groups out there, from non-profit fathers and mothers organizations, single parents groups to chat groups and forums on the Internet. There are wide variations among these groups. Some are serious political organizations, lobbying for changes in the law. Others are simply there to allow individuals in similar situations to connect with one another and share insights and resources. Some are downright lunatic fringe. The only way you find out is to connect with them yourself and trust your instincts about whether or not they are helpful to you. You may well find some extremely useful contacts and resources.

If you find a resource that is particularly outstanding, drop me a line at the address listed under ordering information, and I'll try to include it in later editions.

Part VII

Post
Mortem

45

Will You Be Able to Dance Together at Your Daughter's Wedding?

I realize I have given you a great deal of terrible news. It is not done gratuitously, but with the intent to alert you to the existence of options. I hope that by now you've not only made a firm resolution that if divorce is inevitable, you'll do it right, but have also found some suggestions to help you accomplish that.

There is good news. You *can* be friends with your ex-spouse. Divorce can be done honestly, openly and with dignity on both sides. I have seen clients do it, I have seen friends do it, and I have done it myself. If you do it right, you will be able to dance together at your daughter's wedding. You *might* even dance at your former spouse's wedding. I did. Wouldn't it be wonderful if you could simply remember the good times, embark on a new relationship without feeling the specter of the old one constantly coming between you and your new lover, or watch your spouse get remarried and feel that you are attending the wedding of an old friend?

Not everyone can pull it off, but I am convinced that more people could than do. In many cases, the culprit is that you assume there is no alternative to war and enmity. The simple assumption is that it "*has*" to be that way. It doesn't. Don't let your divorce turn ugly and messy simply because you assume divorce must be ugly and messy. It need not be. It is emotional, painful, and cathartic. I am fond of the zen phrase "Pain is mandatory, but suffering is optional."

Do not start the process assuming that you and your spouse will be sitting across the courtroom from one another. Do not assume that you will have constant ongoing conflicts over your children. Do not assume that you must be adversaries. It is true that your interests and his are no longer the same. However, that does not mean you must have war.

I began this book somewhat sarcastically quoting a common client complaint of "It's not *fair* . . . " This is usually a client's response to being told something he doesn't want to hear. Typically, a person who complains about the lack of fairness is looking for the system, courts, judges or the attorneys to rescue him from the consequences of his own mistakes in judgment. There are thousands of situations which the legal system is simply not designed to redress, and frankly, I wonder whether abstract, absolute fairness even exists. We are all subjective human beings, experiencing our lives (and our divorces) through our own set of filters. Stop looking for abstract fairness, and you will be much more likely to find equity.

If you want your divorce to be fair, then you and your spouse must take responsibility for being fair with one another. The only fairness that you are going to find in the divorce process is the fairness you insist on *from yourself*. Don't look for it out there. Look for it in here.

I had lunch with a colleague recently who casually mentioned that the night before she had attended her son's soccer game and sat with her ex-husband and former father-in-law. The three of them watched the game and had a pleasant conversation with one another. These former spouses do not have an idyllic relationship. They both have complaints about the other, and there have been periods of distinct disagreement since the divorce regarding child-rearing and money issues. Nevertheless, they resolve their differences by talking about them, and they can meet at a soccer game with perfect equanimity. I asked her how she did it and she credited the fact that neither she nor her former husband expected anything else. That's quite revealing. If they expected war, they probably would have had it. They got the divorce they did because that is what they expected of themselves and of each other.

Your friends may be telling you that anger, bitterness and strife are inevitable. They lie. But the only way you will avoid those problems is to fully expect to do so.

Through the course of your divorce, you will have a hundred opportunities to turn it into war. Sometimes the temptation will be almost uncontrollable.

The best thing you can do is be aware. These opportunities come and go and most people are not even conscious that they have a choice, that they can elect to fight or to disengage, to accuse or to detach. If you are not aware that you have a choice, you will not exercise it. Instead, you will simply react. So let your awareness of your options be your first line of defense.

Once you have done that, you will be less likely to opt for the knee-jerk hostile act which plummets you into full-fledged war. If you have done as I suggested and made a list of what is important to you in life, and if you have further reviewed that list periodically, you will have made significant progress. Take your list and devise one or two mental images which symbolize the goal, the ideal end result to you. Perhaps it is as simple as being able to attend the same swim meet or basketball practice as your ex-spouse and be civil to one another for the sake of your child. Perhaps it is the image of being able to dance at your daughter's wedding for your daughter's sake. Or both being at the hospital for the birth of your first grandchild. Whatever it is that speaks to you should be made as vivid as possible. Then, when your awareness tells you that you have a choice of creating peace or war, let this mental image help you make the correct decision.

If you do it right, you can have healthy, well-adjusted children, even if you are the only parent they have. You can get up in the morning and look at yourself in the mirror with pride that you did the best you could under the circumstances at the time. Frankly I don't think we can ask much more than that of ourselves. Your divorce can be a constructive, empowering life passage.

It's your choice.

Glossary

alimony Monetary payments which are made to a spouse or former spouse. This term is used in the federal tax code and in some states. In others, it is being supplanted by the less loaded term "spousal support."

arrearages Unpaid installments of either child or spousal support. In most jurisdictions, they accrue interest at the legal rate until paid.

buy out An agreement whereby one former spouse makes a lump-sum payment to the other in exchange for a waiver of spousal support. When negotiated between the parties, these agreements are enforceable by the courts, but generally cannot be imposed by the court over objection.

consulting attorney An attorney with whom mediating parties consult from time to time to ensure that they understand the legal issues and the consequences of the agreements being discussed.

child support Money payments which are designated for the support of minor children.

custody A term used to designate the parent who has primary responsibility and control over minor children.

> **joint custody** An arrangement whereby each parent has responsibility and control over the children for significant periods. It may or may not represent equal time in each household.
>
> **legal custody** Refers to decision making power over the children. Has little or nothing to do with where the kids actually live or how much time they spend with each parent.

physical custody Refers to the actual place where the children reside. It is not uncommon to see an order for joint legal custody, but primary physical custody to one parent.

shared custody Shared custody is frequently interchangeable with joint custody, and refers to an arrangement where the children spend significant time with each parent.

sole custody Refers to an arrangement where the children primarily reside with one parent, and visit with the other.

split custody In a split custody arrangement, there are two or more children who have different custody and visitation schedules.

discovery The formal legal process by which information and documentation are obtained to prepare a case for settlement or trial. It can include depositions, subpoenas and numerous other methods.

guidelines Either mandatory or discretionary schedules used to determine child or spousal support, based on the income, and sometimes the expenses, of the parents. They vary widely from state to state, and even county to county within a state. Many are computer generated, and frequently the judges have little discretion to depart from them.

jurisdiction As used in this book, it refers to the variations in laws from state to state.

parental alienation An unfortunate situation in which one parent, usually the custodial one, deliberately sets out to alienate the children from the other parent, usually with disastrous results for the mental health and psychological well-being of the children.

pro per An individual who represents himself in a legal proceeding. The term pro se is used in some states.

pro tem A lawyer who is appointed "judge for a day" or for a particular case.

referee Special master. The terms are used virtually interchangeably, depending on the culture of the specific jurisdiction.

special master An individual who is either appointed by the court, or by agreement of the parties, to listen to the evidence and make the decision on a specific issue in the case. Special masters for custody and visitation issues are usually therapists or lawyers by training. Special masters for financial issues may be accountants, attorneys, or retired judges.

support Monetary payments, usually monthly, designated for the support of a spouse or former spouse, or the children. Sometimes called maintenance.

    child support Support which is specifically designated for the children.

    family support Support which is not allocated between child and spousal support. This is usually done for tax purposes, as it can frequently result in increased tax deductions.

    nonmodifiable Support (usually spousal), where the parties have agreed to limit the jurisdiction of the court to modify the amount or the duration, usually in exchange for other concessions.

    spousal Support which is specifically designated for the spouse or former spouse.

tax intercept Federal and state laws which enable a recipient of support to collect unpaid installments by "intercepting" the income tax refund of the payor.

timeshare A less-loaded term than custody to describe the amount of time the children spend in each parent's household.

visitation Refers to the amount of time the children spend with the non-custodial parent.

wage assignment An order which requires the employer to withhold earnings from the payor of support and make the support payment directly to the recipient.

Index

custody 95-102, 257, 177-178, 209
    custody evaluation 80-83, 119-125
    custody evaluators 80-83
    joint custody 95-98, 99, 103-105, 257
    legal custody 257
    physical custody 258
    preparing for an evaluation 122-125
    selecting an evaluator 80-81, 119-122
    shared custody 95-97, 98-100, 258
    sole custody 258
    special masters 88

earnings withholding order, see wage assignment

expert witnesses
    accountants 83-86,
    custody evaluators 80-83
    special masters 86-89, 258
    selecting an accountant 84-86, 88
    selecting a custody evaluator 80-81, 119-122

family support 259

forensic accountants 83-86, See also expert witnesses
    selecting an accountant 84-86, 88

guidelines 133, 137-141, 149-150, 176, 258

judges 38-39, 57-58, 64 See also courts and judges, special masters, referees, private judges

judge pro tem 89, see also private judges

lawyers, see attorneys

maintenance, see alimony, spousal support

About the Author

M. Sue Talia has been a practicing family lawyer in Danville, California, since 1977. She is a Family Law Specialist, certified by the Board of Legal Specialization of the State Bar of California. Her focus is on complex family law litigation. She obtained her B.A. from Santa Clara University, her M.A. from Stanford University, and J.D. from the University of California, Hastings College of the Law.

In addition to the practice of law, she teaches workshops for family lawyers, forensic accountants and individuals contemplating divorce.

She has long been active in legal and community organizations, is a founding director of the Family Law Section of the Contra Costa Bar Association, and is currently involved in efforts to restructure the California family law courts to make them more responsive to the needs of children and families.

Did you borrow this book?

Want a copy of your own?

Please send _____ copies of *How to Avoid the Divorce from Hell (and Dance Together at Your Daughter's Wedding)* at $12.95 per copy. Please add $3.00 per book for postage and handling. California residents include sales tax of 7.25% (or other local rate). Allow 30 days for delivery.

Send check payable to Nexus Publishing Company to 480 San Ramon Valley Boulevard, Suite A, Box 257, Danville, CA 94526.

Call credit card orders to 1-800-393-0751 or fax to (510) 743-1614.

Name _____

Phone (_____) _____

Address_____

City _____ State_____ Zip_____

Enclosed is my check/money order for $_____

Bill my   VISA_____   MasterCard_____

Account No. _____ Expires _____

Signature _____

Quantity Orders Invited